D1638225

# Living Sacrifice

# Living Sacrifice

by

## Helen M. Roseveare

HODDER AND STOUGHTON
LONDON SYDNEY AUCKLAND TORONTO

British Library Cataloguing in Publication Data

Roseveare, Helen
    Living sacrifice.
    1. Roseveare, Helen
    2. Missions, Medical – Zaire – Biography
    I. Title
    266′.025′0924         BV3625.C63R633

ISBN 0 340 23765 1

*First published 1979*

*Copyright © 1979 by Helen M. Roseveare*

*Printed in Great Britain for
Hodder and Stoughton Ltd.,
Mill Road, Dunton Green, Sevenoaks, Kent
by Cox & Wyman Ltd., London, Reading and Fakenham*

# Contents

# Foreword and Dedication

I WAS CONVERTED through the work of the Cambridge Women's Inter-Collegiate Christian Union (CWICCU, branch of IVF as it was then, UCCF of to-day) in 1945, and taught by them the habit of daily Bible Study.

I learned the joy of Christian service with the Bromley Class of the Girl Crusaders' Union (GCU), teaching a Saturday and Sunday girls' Bible Class from 1946 to 1950: I have been an associate member of the Union ever since.

I have served as a medical missionary with the Worldwide Evangelization Crusade (WEC) in Congo/Zaire from 1953 to 1973, and on their home staff since then, enjoying the privileges of deep fellowship in the family.

I wish to express my heartfelt gratitude to the older members of these three organisations for all they have taught me (however inadequately I have learned the lessons) of a life of sacrifice in Christ's service.

My desire in writing this small book is to pass on these lessons to others "who hunger and thirst for righteousness" not as though I had already attained, but that together we may press on towards maturity in being made conformable to our Master.

*Note*: All Biblical references are quoted from the RSV unless otherwise stated.

# PROLOGUE

# His right to demand

*I appeal to you therefore, brethren, by the mercies of God, to present your bodies as a living sacrifice, holy and and acceptable to God, which is your spiritual worship.*
ROM. 12: 1

IT WAS COLD as we trudged from the bus-stop to the church, the lightly falling snow muffling our footfalls and adding to our sense of loneliness. In the large empty church, the flickering candle light hardly penetrated the darkness of that early December morning, as I knelt, a shivering seven-year-old, beside the quiet figure of my Mother. She had come to thank God for the birth of another little sister into our family. I did not fully understand why we were there, and yet in a strange way, I knew it was right.

The verger turned the lights on, and I closed my eyes to shut out the hard glare, and to retreat back into the mystery of darkness.

The minister was praying. I glanced up at Mother: her face looked lovely and her eyes shone. I tried to listen, to understand, but I was shivering and felt afraid. Mother put an arm round me and drew me closer to herself, and suddenly I knew that she needed me, and I loved her. I followed her finger in the prayer book, and we were praying together. The rector's voice was hushed and barely audible as he prepared for the communion service. For perhaps the first time, my restless spirit was stilled momentarily by a sense of the Presence of God.

"We are not worthy ..." reached through to my under-standing, and made me feel guilty. I shrank yet closer to Mother.

"Almighty God, our heavenly Father, who of Thy tender mercy didst give Thine only Son Jesus Christ to suffer death upon the Cross for our redemption: who made there (by His one oblation of Himself once offered) a full, perfect, and sufficient sacrifice, oblation and satisfaction for the sins of the whole world; and ...".

Mother had forgotten her seven-year-old, her heart and mind drawing strength and comfort from the well-known prayer. She ceased to point ... and no longer listening, I re-read that beautiful phrase that seemed underlined by her stationary finger.

She moved away from me, up to the communion rail.

"The body of our Lord Jesus Christ, which was given for thee, preserve thy body and soul unto everlasting life. Take and eat this in remembrance that Christ died for thee, and feed on Him in thy heart by faith with thanks-giving."

*"Christ died for thee."* For a brief second, in that solemn moment of awed silence, I heard the Spirit say those words to me, in my heart.

The moment passed. Scarf wound tightly round my neck, beret and knitted mitts pulled on against the damp winter chill, I followed Mother out of the quiet church, and we made our way home.

"Mummy, what is an oblation?"

Perhaps she was startled out of her own line of thought, taken by surprise, or perhaps she just did not know. Maybe the question jarred against the stirrings of faith, making her question that which she wanted to accept. I do not remem-ber what she answered, except that it seemed short and curt.

For some reason, deep inside of me, I felt hurt, so I did not ask again, yet I needed to know the answer.

I found her prayer book later that day, and the marker was in the Communion Service. Slowly, laboriously, I found my way through to that particular prayer, and read and re-read the first paragraph. I learnt it by heart. For months, I used to recite it to myself in bed at night before falling asleep. The words had a beauty, a fascination, that reached down towards an inner need: yet so much was incomprehensible. What was redemption? What was an oblation? I looked the words up in a dictionary, but the flat explanations spoilt the mystery of the incomprehensible.

It was many years later before I gave in to the promptings of the Spirit, to realise that God had so loved *me* that He had given His only Son Jesus Christ to suffer death on the Cross for *my* redemption – to save me from my sins, to take upon Himself my punishment and all that I deserved.

"A full, perfect and sufficient sacrifice, oblation and satisfaction for the sins of the whole world" was made by Christ at Calvary, because He loved us.

The mystery of that great Sacrifice still stirs my soul to its depths. That the Son of God could so love me that He would give Himself for me, still stirs a sense of awed wonder.

There was no other good enough to pay the price of sin:
He only could unlock the gate of heaven and let us in.

The well-known words of childhood hymns became more precious, more meaningful, as one sought to enter into an understanding of the Mystery.

If He so loved me that He was willing to die for me, whatever could I do for Him even to begin to show my heart's longing to thank Him? "A full, perfect and sufficient Sacrifice" – sufficient, sufficient for the sin of the whole world. So no more could be offered. The only possible acceptable sacrifice was complete. Christ had sacrificed Himself, once for all – once for all time, once for all people, once for all sin. No further sacrifice was needed or possible. God had shown Himself satisfied by that perfect offering, when He brought back the Lord Jesus Christ from the dead, raising Him to life again that first Easter morning. I could add nothing to the efficacy of His sacrifice: I could do nothing to save myself from the penalty of my sins. He had done it all.

Yet there was a striving in my inner being to do something to express my heart's response to His great love for me. His Spirit in me stirred that unrest, planting in my heart the desire to respond to an insistent demand made upon me by that "one oblation of Himself once offered."

*       *       *

Paul, a nine-year old African school-boy, grabbed by a rebel soldier and struck across the face, flung on the ground, brutally kicked and beaten with the butt end of a gun, refused to give in to intimidation.

This incident occurred during the civil uprising in the Congo in 1964. Paul had to make a choice. He could have escaped, but that might have led to the capture of others. Young as he was, he had had to think out, quickly and decisively, a course of action, knowing that the alternative to escape put him in a position of considerable personal danger. He may not have known just how great that danger was, but he was no fool, and he knew it would include physical pain. He had already seen others beaten, threatened . . .

He could still hear the piteous screams of that woman and her teenage daughter that the rebels had captured in the maternity compound of the hospital. He had been in school that morning when a truckload of armed gangsters had driven into the village. A wild, dark-eyed youth with a blank face of sullen hatred, armed with a spear, had rushed into the school compound, and ordered them all to stand. Another was doing the same in the church, next door to Paul's classroom. Six or more others had charged over to the maternity compound, through the child-welfare clinic, through the wards, out to the special care unit, across to the orphanage home. Noise, shouts, anger. Then they had returned with these two women as captives, the sixteen-year-old girl with swollen puffy eyes from sleepless nights of fear, and her mother, seven months with child, even then in pain. They had been unceremoniously thrown up into the truck: then the girl beaten and bullied and taken down, forced into the cab to direct them to the place where her father was in hiding. He was apparently a paid secretary of the national government, the "last regime", and therefore to be shot by the present rebel regime. As the truck had lurched off, the mother had fallen; and Paul had heard her piteous screams as the soldiers jeeringly kicked her.

His mind raced back to that other occasion, the week before. So much had happened since, it seemed years away. He had been asleep between his two brothers, when he was woken by a gun-shot somewhere outside in the dark. He sat bolt upright and saw the front door crash open, and Susan, one of the senior nurses, rush through the house naked, slamming the door behind her. He had raced after her, wildly terrified, no idea what was happening. She had flung herself over the palisade behind the home, and he had not been able to follow her. He had crouched back in the vegetable plot, whimpering and scared, as soldiers had searched round his home, shouting and angry. He had not understood.

He just knew it was all evil, and unreasonable, and no-one was safe from their wickedness.

During the first eight weeks of the rebellion, the guerilla soldiers had forced the National Army back over nearly four-fifths of the country. All rebel troops were subjected to initiation rites by the witch-doctors, and thereby considered "protected" against the bullets of the government forces, which would "turn to water" as they surged forward in the name of their martyred hero, Patrice Lumumba.

Then came the day when the President of the Republic accepted the help of Colonel Mike Hoare and white mercenary soldiers. The tide turned. Discipline in the National Army improved, morale rose, and the rebels were forced to begin their long retreat. Battle after battle raged, and hundreds of rebel soldiers were killed.

In desperation, the guerilla army began drafting sixteen-year-old school boys into their depleted ranks, giving them a few days' drilling, initiation rites and arm-bands. We saw trucks drive through our village, laden with singing youths, "off to the war". Hardly any came back. We heard terrible rumours of the massacre at the front, the war cry of the young zealots "Mayi – mayi – Lumumba!" mingling with the agonised screams of their dying companions, mowed down by a superior force of arms.

On the 23rd October, the guerillas rounded up three hundred fourteen-year-olds from the local Roman Catholic school. It would be our turn next. How could we protect our teenagers? We could not send them home as more than half of them were our own orphanage children. This *was* their home.

A contingency plan was drawn up to safeguard as many as possible in the event of a direct attack on the school. Each morning, two village workmen were nominated as scouts.

They went to the north and south ends of the village and hid in the undergrowth at the roadside. Should they hear in the distance the sound of an approaching vehicle, they were to whistle a sharp alarm signal. (By then, all vehicles in the area were in the hands of the rebel forces.) The first in the village to hear the whistled warning was to beat a quick message on the talking drum, and all knew what to do next. Action had to be immediate. There would be barely four minutes from the sound of the whistle to the arrival of the soldiers.

In the school, each of the five masters was to lead his class of twenty to thirty children down into the relative safety of the forest behind the village. They could go on any pretext they liked, such as a botany or nature study walk, for a games or gymnastic period, but they were to keep the youngsters happy and quiet, as far from the village as possible, till we signalled them to return.

A monitor was to be appointed weekly in each class, whose job was to gather up all school material, books and pencils, blackboard chalk and rubber, into a provided basket: and to push the desks and benches haphazardly into disarray, as though the building had not been used since the previous school year, four months ago. Hurrying over to my house with their laden baskets, they were to put them in a big cupboard, open and ready, the last one closing the door, and to run after their classmates, down to the forest – all within the four-minute warning period.

One day, suddenly, the whistles blew: the drum beat out its staccato warning: the masters set off for the forest with their young charges: the monitors hurriedly cleared the school. Nine-year-old Paul was fourth-grade monitor that week. Small for his age, the son of leprosy parents, he had difficulty in reaching up to unpin charts attached to the blackboard frame. He dragged a bench up from the classroom, but still could not reach. He rushed for a second bench, and precariously tried to balance it on the first. Scrambling up without upsetting them, tears of frustration pricked his eyes, as, nervously struggling with the stubborn drawing pins, he saw the other monitors crossing the courtyard with their filled baskets.

At last, Paul was ready. As he was leaving the school, lugging the ungainly basket, the other four monitors were disappearing into the forest. He could hear the approaching truck. It down-geared to take the sharp corner as it passed through the village, still out of sight, over the brow of the hill. Then Paul heard the rev-up, as the truck swung round to come up into the village courtyard. He was caught!

Every instinct told him to drop the basket and run.

Yet in the same instant, another thought flashed into his mind. The basket would be right in the pathway of the truck, and it contained exercise books with to-day's date! The soldiers were bound to see them, and then they would know that there really was a school, despite every effort to disguise the fact. All would have been in vain. Worse than in vain, in fact. They would search till they found the pupils ... and young Paul was astute enough to know that the punishment meted out for hiding would be added to their original planned wickedness, had they been found in the classrooms.

Heart pounding with fear, Paul struggled for a second in indecision.

What was that story he had heard recently in Sunday School, of a twelve-year-old girl in Communist China? She had been caught by the Red Guards as she came out of a house, where they suspected an underground church. Held for three days for interrogation, she was brought out before a people's court eventually. Challenged directly by the guards, she knew it was a question of life or death.

"Do you love Jesus?"

Poised to say "No", caught in a vice of fear, she saw a girl of her own age down in the crowd silently make the sign of the cross.

Drawing herself erect, she proudly answered: "Yes, I love Jesus."

And they shot her.

"If she could, I can," said Paul to himself, through gritted teeth.

He struggled across the courtyard, over the verandah, and pushed the basket into the front room. There was no time to spare: the truck was already in the drive. Paul pulled the double doors shut, and leaning against them, he turned to face the soldiers.

The guerillas piled out of the truck, cruel and determined. They spread out in every direction, searching for what and whom they wanted. Two came to my home and shouted roughly at Paul.

"Wanafunzi ni wapi?" (Where are your classmates?)

Almost paralysed with fear, Paul could not answer. He bit his lip to control the rising panic. In his heart, he prayed to God for courage to go through with it, and that he might know what to do or say. Only nine – could God help him? He had only come to know the Lord Jesus as his Saviour a few months previously. Certainly there was no-one else who could help him now. The fingers of his right hand, frantically twisting in his clenched left fist behind his back, pressed the deaf-and-dumb signal "P-M": "P-M", as his lips soundlessly formed the precious formula "piem" over and over again.*

---

* The secret code of Paul's youth group, P-M, stood for "Pasipo Mupaka", part of the motto, "Kwa Yeye pasipo mupaka", "For HIM (Jesus Christ) with no limits."

They grabbed him, flung him to the cement floor, beat him and kicked him. Dragging him to his feet, they repeated their question angrily.

Suddenly Paul knew what he had to do. His mind cleared, his fear dropped away. Jackie, a boy in his class, was a deaf-mute who could only communicate by garbled sounds and gesticulations. Paul pretended to be Jackie, and mouthed an inarticulate answer to the soldiers.

"Don't dare mock us," they screamed in unreasoning rage, flinging Paul again roughly to the ground and ruthlessly kicking him in their frustrated fury. "Tell us where they are hiding."

As they dragged Paul to his feet, the boy, filled with new-found courage, went through the charade a second time.

"Under my breath," he told me later, "I kept repeating 'P-M, P-M, P-M,' to remind myself that Jesus loved me so much that He died for me, and so I could go through anything they did to me, for His sake."

Suddenly one soldier said: "We're wasting time. This boy must be a deaf-mute. He cannot help us."

Throwing the lad back against the closed doors, they left the verandah to join their comrades, gathering from various directions. Two came back from the school buildings.

"There's no school here. The place is in chaos, and obviously hasn't been used for months."

Climbing into the truck, they drove off.

Returning from the hospital where I had been on duty, I came into my home through the back door. Entering the sitting room, I was surprised to see the double doors closed. As I pulled them open, Paul fell into the room. The lad had been severely beaten, and was very shaken. I lifted him up and carried him to the settee. Getting us both hot drinks, I

asked him what had happened. Slowly, sipping his choco-
late, he told me. Then looking up, he asked:

"Have the soldiers gone, Doctor?"

"Yes, Paul, they've gone."

"Did they find the other school boys?"

"No, Paul, they didn't."

"Did I save them, Doctor?"

"Yes, Paul, you did."

There was a moment's pause. Glancing up at me, the lad
said simply and very sincerely: "No, Doctor, it wasn't really
me, was it? It was the Lord Jesus in me."

\* \* \*

Paul had come to know the Lord Jesus as his friend and
Saviour only a short time before. It had been at a Youth
Rally. The visiting evangelist had spoken, in the closing epilogue, of our Lord's return as King and Judge. He had
asked the children if they would be ready to meet and greet
the Lord with joy, or if they would try to run away and hide
their faces in shame.

"Have you anything in your heart or life of which you
would be ashamed, if the Lord Jesus came right now?"

Paul had gone home very quietly, with a miserable feeling
inside. Next morning, as his father read the Bible and
prayed with the family, before going out to work, Paul had
started to cry, and eventually blurted out: "I couldn't meet
Him: I'd be ashamed!"

His father quietened him, and got him to explain his out-
burst. Then, encouraged by his parents, he had confessed all
that was in his young heart to the Lord, and had asked
God's forgiveness, and that Jesus would save him, and come
to live in his heart.

Now when this test had come, faced by the cruelty of the

rebel soldiers, Paul had hardly hesitated. God's love for him and in him had dictated the action he had taken: and he was glad. He had found a way to express to God his great love for Him. He had not thought it out like that: he did not even reason it out after it was all over. But he had peace and joy in his heart: and he knew more wholly than before how much he did love his Saviour.

Had God the right to demand of Paul that willingness to sacrifice himself to save his school fellows? Had He the right to demand such a demonstration of love? Can one question God's rights, or His ultimate purpose and motive? Perhaps God was not demanding a demonstration of love, but rather offering to Paul a privileged opportunity of sharing in his love? God Himself so loved Paul that He had given His only begotten Son to die in his place to redeem him: now they had shared together in a demonstration of that love for others.

Is there always a *cost* involved in responding to that insistent demand in our hearts to express to Him our love? Would I be willing to pay such a cost, perhaps a similar price to Paul's, if asked to do so? Do I believe that as my Saviour, He has the right to demand such a response to His love, if I would really love Him as He first loved me?

Peter, when the Lord told His disciples that that same night all would desert Him, had boldly declared that he would never do so. He would rather die than desert Him. The test came, and Peter failed miserably, denying the Lord with oaths. Fear had made a coward of him. The *cost* of loving the Lord wholly in that instant had seemed too great to pay.

Momentarily I had felt the same the night the rebel soldiers first took me captive. Beaten, flung on the ground, kicked – teeth broken, mouth and nose gashed, ribs bruised

– driven at gun point back to my home, jeered at, insulted, threatened – I knew that if the rebel lieutenant did not pull the trigger of his revolver and end the situation, worse pain and humiliation lay ahead. It was a very dark night. I felt unutterably alone. For a brief moment, I felt God had failed me. He could have stepped in and prevented this rising crescendo of wickedness and cruelty. He could have saved me out of their hands. Why didn't He speak? Why didn't He intervene? And in desperation, I almost cried out against Him: "It is too much to pay!"

Yet His love for me cost Him His life. He gave Himself, in that one all-sufficient atoning Sacrifice at Calvary. He so loved that He gave all. His Sacrifice was the expression of His great love.

But His sacrifice had achieved something. He had saved lost mankind from their sins. What was I achieving by suffering brutality at the hands of rebel soldiers? If I died (which seemed probable and imminent) no-one would even know of the suffering. What was being gained? God, why, why?

In the darkness and loneliness, He met with me. He was right there, a great, wonderful, almighty God. His love enveloped me. Suddenly the "Why?" dropped away from me, and an unbelievable peace flowed in, even in the midst of the wickedness. And He breathed a word into my troubled mind: the word Privilege.

"These are not your sufferings: they are not beating you. These are My sufferings: all I ask of you is the loan of your body."

For twenty years, anything I had needed, I had asked of God and He had provided. Now, this night, the Almighty had stooped to ask of *me* something that He condescended to appear to need, and He offered me the PRIVILEGE of responding. He wanted my body, in which to live, and through which to love these very rebel soldiers in the height of their wickedness. It was inconceivable, yet true. He offered me the inestimable privilege of sharing with Him in some little measure, at least, in the edge of the fellowship of His sufferings. And it was all privilege.

For that night, cost became swallowed up in privilege.

What is cost, anyway? At best, it is only a relative term, with no absolute value. It can be understood only in reference to the object desired, and its value may change according to circumstances. A sack of rice for ten pounds sterling would seem dear in normal conditions, but the cost would be immaterial in conditions of starvation.

Early on in my missionary life in Africa, God taught me a lesson as to the meaning of *cost* in relation to what He wanted to do in my life, to make me more like the Lord Jesus Christ. The palm trees in our village of Nebobongo were being stripped of leaves by an invasion of small, brightly coloured, weaver birds, and this was affecting the yield of urgently needed oil from the palm nuts, a basic commodity in both our local diet and also the local industrial economy.

I offered the children of the village a penny for every bird shot. (Later, as they became excellent marksmen, and the invasion continued unabated, the offer was changed to ten birds for a penny!) From then on, we noticed apparently wanton destruction of the lower boughs of flowering acacia trees, of red-leaved poinsettia shrubs, of blossom-bearing branches of coffee bushes, of fruit-laden branches of orange and grapefruit trees. The latter really stung us into an active search for the culprits.

Not far to find! Everywhere we found children whittling away at branches from any accessible tree or bush, using any available weapon as knife, to create arrows. Even in the back row of the classroom, during a maths lesson, I heard the inescapable tell-tale sound of sand-papering, as a banana-leaf was rubbed energetically up and down a stripped stem to polish an amazingly straight arrow shaft, for the all-important, new, financially fruitful hobby of archery!

We had to weigh up the comparative "costs". We needed oranges and grapefruit in our diet, so those trees became banned to the amateur archers. We sold coffee beans to augment our hospital funds, so those bushes were forbidden. But we decided the beauty afforded by the bright yellow blossoms and feathery green leaves of the acacia trees was only appreciated by the white foreigners. The branches were not even of value for firewood. The "cost" as measured by the acacia trees was decidedly less than that caused by the loss of the palm leaves through the destruction by the weaver birds. From then on, bright yellow acacia blossoms and feathery green leaves could be found littered all over the paths of the village, the price paid for the construction of arrows to destroy the destructive birds.

So the Lord spoke directly to me about what He wanted to do in my life. I personally had liked the bright yellow acacia trees. They broke up, for me, the monotony of green that shrouds the great rain forests. But we needed the palm oil. The one was relinquished for the other. The bright flowers and leaves were sacrificed to make the needed arrows. There was nothing wrong with the flowers and leaves. In fact, they were essential for the life and reproduction of the trees. Yet they were not only unnecessary, they were definitely a hindrance for an arrow. The side branches, thorns and knots needed smoothing off. It seemed that each branch became impersonalised, losing its own particular form and beauty, sacrificed for the one aim of producing a straight, well-balanced arrow. Even the bark had to be stripped off, leaving the stem naked, exposed to wind and rain. The branch as such had been destroyed. It could no longer feed or reproduce: its beauty had been vandalised. It could no longer be recognised for itself; and even its power to survive in all weathers would be challenged.

This wanton act of destruction might seem a senseless waste of God-given beauty. It might be measured as a high price to pay to allow children the fun of making bows and arrows. Yet if from the destructive process, the polished shaft of the arrow that emerged was able to rid the community of hordes of preying birds, preserving for us an essential source of health-producing food, would not the "cost" seem more acceptable?

"Therefore, since we are surrounded by so great a cloud of witnesses, let us also lay aside every weight, and sin which clings so closely, and let us run with perseverance the race that is set before us, looking to Jesus, the pioneer and perfecter of our faith, who for the joy that was set before Him, endured the Cross, despising the shame, and is seated at the right hand of the throne of God" (Hebrews 12: 1, 2).

Could I see that God wanted to transform my life from a somewhat ugly useless branch to an arrow, a tool usable in His hands, for the furtherance of His purposes? It was said of the Lord Jesus Christ: "The Lord called Me from the womb, from the body of My Mother He named My Name. He made My mouth like a sharp sword, in the shadow of His hand He hid Me; He made Me *a polished arrow*, in His quiver He hid Me away: and He said to Me, 'You are My Servant, Israel, in whom I will be glorified' " (Isaiah 49: 1–3).

To be thus transformed, was I willing – am I still willing – for the whittling, sand-papering, stripping processes necessary in my Christian life? The ruthless pulling off of leaves and flowers might include the doing-without a television set or washing machine, the remaining single in order to see a job done, the re-evaluation of the worthiness of the ambition to be a "good" doctor (according to *my* terms and values). The snapping off of thorns might include drastic dealing with hidden jealousies and unknown prides, the giving up of prized rights in leadership and administration. The final stripping of the bark might include lessons to be learned regarding death to self – self-defence, self-pity, self-justification and vindication, self-sufficiency, all the mechanisms of preventing the hurt of too-deep involvement. Am I prepared for the pain, that may at times seem like sacrifice, in order to be made into a tool in His service? My willingness will be a measure of the sincerity of my desire to express my heart-felt gratitude to Him for His so-great salvation.

Can I see such minor "sacrifices" in the light of the great Sacrifice of Calvary where Christ gave all for me? Can I see the apparent cost as minimal compared to the reality of the gain? Do I accept His right to demand my willingness to pay such a price, in order to enter into the privilege and joy of being used in His purposes?

God so loved me that He gave all, His very Self, to redeem me.

How can I love Him in like manner? How can I show Him that love?

"He who has My commandments and keeps them, he it is who loves Me" (John 14: 21).

What are His commandments, that I must obey, to show Him my love?

Jesus answered: "The first is, 'Hear, O Israel, The Lord our God, the Lord is One: and you shall love the Lord your

God with all your heart, and with all your soul, and with all your mind, and with all your strength.' The second is this, 'You shall love your neighbour as yourself.' There is no other commandment greater than these" (Mark 12: 29-31).

To love the Lord my God with ALL my heart will involve a spiritual cost. I'll have to give Him my heart, and let Him love through it whom and how He wills, even if this seems at times to break my heart.

To love the Lord my God with ALL my soul will involve a volitional and emotional cost. I'll have to give Him my will, my rights to decide and choose, and all my relationships, for Him to guide and control, even when I cannot understand His reasoning.

To love the Lord my God with ALL my mind will involve an intellectual cost. I must give Him my mind, my intelligence, my reasoning powers, and trust Him to work through them, even when He may appear to act in contradiction to common sense.

To love the Lord my God with ALL my strength will involve a physical cost. I must give Him my body to indwell, and through which to speak, whether He chooses by health or sickness, by strength or weakness, and trust Him utterly with the outcome.

The sum of these apparent costs (as with the stripping of the branch to create the arrow) could be considered as the sacrifice that I am invited to offer Him as the response of my whole being to His love for me in that one "full perfect and sufficient Sacrifice, oblation and satisfaction for the sins of the whole world". It is my way of expressing my gratitude to Christ for all He is, and for all He has done and given for me.

## Chapter 1

# With ALL my heart

*A new heart I will give you, and a new spirit I will put within you: and I will take out of your flesh the heart of stone and give you a heart of flesh.*

EZEK. 36: 26

HOW MUCH I learned in those early months in Africa! First, one had to tackle the language. Our missionary society was working in an area of some fifty thousand square miles, where 18 different major tribal groups lived. These tribes consisted of eight to eighty thousand people, each with a language completely distinct from its neighbour. Only three or four of these languages had yet been reduced to writing. Throughout the area, two trade languages had grown up to provide a means of inter-tribal communications, Bangala to the north and Kingwana (now Swahili Zaire) to the south. Ibambi, our central village where I lived at first, was on the border area between the two trade languages, and to communicate at all freely, one needed to know both these.

I had travelled the five week journey from England to Ibambi with two missionary couples returning after furlough. From them, on board ship, I had my first language lessons. As we slowly steamed down the Suez canal, it was hard to concentrate on the eight classes of nouns in the Swahili language, with the diversion of a train of camels just a few yards away! Fortunately for me, Swahili is a phonetic, non-tonal language that obeys definite rules and is relatively easy to learn. Plunged into work on arrival, I was forced to use the little I knew, and so made rapid strides.

Adapting to culture and new dietary regimes was honestly little of a problem to me. I was so excited to be there and wanted to become one with the people as fast as I could, that I noticed no barrier or sense of shock. Maybe our fairly rigorous upbringing during the rationing shortages of World War Two, and having spent most of childhood's holidays camping or mountaineering, was a real help in developing an adaptability to any circumstances. And I was so thrilled to have arrived in Africa, I would have enjoyed practically anything.

Clinic work for seemingly endless crowds of very sick people filled every day. They never ceased to come. The little room where I worked under a corrugated iron roof was always full and always hot and always noisy. The heat and noise and numbers were appalling. I felt I would never get accustomed to THIS. The huge grotesque stinking ulcers that had eaten away at bodies already thin from malnutrition had to be seen to be believed. The racking coughs, the swollen pus-filled eyes, the violent intestinal problems, almost overwhelmed me. The countless women with their heads tightly bound with a vine-string to attempt to control a splitting head-ache, the hot tired sweaty bodies burning with malarial fever, were incredible. Babies, desperately thin, with pale staring eyes and bloated stomachs, tore at my heart continuously.

Would I ever get used to the NEED? And the pathetic gratitude of the people for anything I could do for them. They loved me: they really did.

One evening, a young boy arrived at Ibambi, with a scrawled note on a piece of paper torn from a school ex-

ercise book. His father, a village catechist, was ill and unable
to get to us. Would I go to see him, please, and take him
medicine?

The African, who would normally have driven me there,
was sick. Not only did I not know the way, but I had not as
yet begun driving on the rough dirt roads. Jack Scholes, my
missionary leader, offered to drive me to the village, and this
gave him the opportunity for a talk with me.

"Helen," he said quietly, looking straight ahead between
the walls of elephant grass over the central grass-tufted
mound of the dirt-track road: "if you think you have come
to the Mission field because you are a little better than
others, because you have more to offer through your medical training, or . . ." There was nothing censorious in his
tone, yet his words cut deeply into my heart. Was that the
appearance that I had given to others, of a spiritual
superiority, that I knew all the answers and would show
them how the job should be done? Had I been so busy
tackling the NEEDS of the bodies of those who came for
help, that I had had little or no time, and no inclination to
make time, for fellowship with other members of the team?
Did I subconsciously feel that my service to the community
through medicine would bring more people to the Saviour
than these others had done by years of patient trekking and
preaching?

A wave of shame and a sense of failure came over me. I
tried not to reply, as a sense of self-pity made itself felt. Why
did they misunderstand me? Why did no-one appreciate
how hard I was working, how tired I was, how much I
needed fellowship and support? No-one offered to help me,
or relieve me on night duty. The "pity-poor-little-me" syn-
drome started early in my missionary career.

"Remember," Jack concluded, "the Lord has only one

main purpose ultimately in each of our lives, that is, to make us more like our Lord Jesus."

As we talked over the implications of what he was saying, he suggested to me that the next thing God wanted to do in my life to make me more like Jesus, He could not do for me back in Britain, as I was too stubborn and wilful: so He had brought me to Africa, to work in me through Africans.

Another voice spoke quite clearly: "to make you realise and face up to this 'pity-poor-little-me' attitude, and become real," and I turned my head away.

It all seemed such revolutionary teaching. So simple and childlike, it was nevertheless so profound and deeply disturbing. It put all "missionary" work into a new perspective and made me feel very small.

I began to feel the pressures of the medical work. There were so many sick and ill needing help, and so little we could do for them. There was so little space. I needed an examination room where I could be quiet, away from the throng, able to listen to chests and hearts, and to think concisely what could be done for each patient. I needed a pharmacy, for stocking medical supplies, making up mixtures, dispensing drugs to patients through a hatch or some such arrangement. I needed wards where I could care for the more gravely ill, with a section for maternity cases, and another section for isolation. I drew up plans, but it was hard to be simple enough to be realistic. I asked the fellowship's permission and encouragement to start building. The church agreed, and work commenced on a large mud and thatch erection to be divided up for a multi-purpose building for women patients. The work was so slow! It rained almost every day, and one does not work in the rain in the tropics! We waited for the poles: we waited for the vines: we waited for thatch. Then we waited for window and door frames:

we waited for lime to plaster the walls: we waited ...

It took just over a year. Meanwhile the work went on in our small overcrowded clinic. A workman at the Mission printing press developed acute mastoiditis. We had no antibiotics in the early fifties: they could actually be obtained at the nearest pharmacy-store fifty miles north but only at an exorbitant cost. The money we had available was needed to pay the workmen on the site. We stopped work there for a week to buy two small bottles of penicillin. Dared one incise the bulging abscess? The book told me how and where, but I'd never seen it done. The book also warned of all the dangers. We prayed: I incised: the penicillin worked: God touched and the man recovered.

Another man died the following week of the same disease, and I felt sick.

A baby was brought in, severely burned. Over half the surface area of the body had been scorched with boiling palm fat. The text book warned that cure was impossible. The shock would kill the baby. We laid the baby in the canvas bag I used as a bath in my home, and soaked the body in warm water with bicarbonate of soda, borrowed from a missionary's kitchen. I carefully cut the blisters with boiled-up embroidery scissors. We attempted to sterilise strips of gauze in a biscuit tin over a wood fire, and wrapped all in a clean, brightly coloured, knitted blanket. The baby was laid in a wooden box, on a straw-stuffed mattress, covered with butter-muslin to keep out mosquitoes and flies. The baby did well, I remember, and recovered.

I could not sleep, I was so anxious about the needs around me. What more could I be doing?

A man, a catechist from an out-lying church, was carried in, gravely ill with a strangulated hernia. The four bearers had been walking eight days to reach us. I did not do

B

surgery then. I was untrained. It would be unethical to attempt to learn to do operations under the prevailing conditions – so I thought then. He was carried on to a Belgian Red Cross hospital, but he died during the operation.

The first group of African students, who had already gathered round me for training, looked at me accusingly when the news reached us. Their looks said: If we'd operated here, he might have lived.

I did not sleep that night. My heart was tortured with pain. I could not do more. I did not know how to do more. I was not willing to attempt to do more. Slowly the force of my violent arguments lessened, and I realised that God was saying that we should and would do more.

A wee premature baby was carried to us, about four days old. It looked like a drowned rat. I have never seen anything so tiny and yet alive. But it was all skin and bone. I turned away with a sickening sense of hopelessness. The baby needed careful incubator care, with controlled drip feeding. Oh, yes, I knew the answers: I knew what the book said. But how?

It was pouring with rain. That was the first time that I ran out into a downpour, and placed a table in the middle of the courtyard away from all over-hanging trees. Hurrying back, I collected a clean cloth and all the glass-ware I could quickly find and placed all on the table. Twenty minutes later, as the storm abated, the students watching me in mystified silence from the protection of the covered verandah, I collected everything again. Measuring a litre of rain water in a clean saucepan, I boiled it with a heaped spoonful of table salt, and strained it through six layers of gauze bandage. Armed with a syringe, and my litre of saline, I took a student into a second room, with the tiny scrap of a baby held in the hand of a tribal woman. I showed the student how to give slow subcutaneous injections of 5ml. of saline at a time, under the loose folds of skin. He continued throughout the day. Another student dropped sugar solution from a syringe into the baby's gasping mouth, drop by drop, minute by minute, through two days and nights. The baby lived.

Could one keep going? It was not the physical strain alone that was telling on me, but the emotional trauma as well. Day after day, night after night, my heart was torn with the burdens and the needs. Besides which, they all expected me to be able to cope, able to invent, able to improvise. They were all so grateful for anything I did, whether successful or not. My heart was numbed from carrying their burdens.

Then the night came, when a new-born baby, apparently healthy, died in the maternity care centre. It was the first time that I had been faced with this, and somehow, something drawn taut inside me snapped. I could bear no more.

I had been called at about 2 a.m., by a tap on my bedroom window by a frightened pupil midwife, frightened by the dark, by the fear of evil spirits, by the nearness of death.

I dressed rapidly and ran across to the ward. The baby did not move or cry. I tried to resuscitate it, mouth-to-mouth breathing. I held the slack body against my own body to give it warmth. The baby was dead. There was nothing I could do. The others there had already tried all that I was trying to do and they stood watching me, wearily, in an uneasy silence. I was suddenly, unreasonably, angry. I snapped at the missionary midwife:

"Why didn't you send for me earlier?"

The implication was obvious: and she in turn, hurt and angry, turned on the senior African midwife, and demanded: "Why didn't YOU call ME earlier?"

The ball was passed from court to court, as the senior mid-wife repeated the accusing question to the pupil, and she to the relative of the mother. We ended up in the despairing situation of apparently blaming the mother for the death of her own baby. There was a terrible silence. I left the ward and went back home, sullen in the loneliness of a responsible job. I knew at once that my anger had been unjustified, and that I should not have asked the offensive question. In my heart I knew that I had to carry the final responsibility, that I could not pass it back to others. "Passing the buck" really only goes in one direction, and in our medical service, I was the end of the line. But I was angry. Against whom? I didn't know. Against the system perhaps: against my own frus-trating inadequacy and lack of experience and of skill: against the lot of the people where I lived and whom I was growing to love, in their abject poverty. None of this helped the situation.

For three days there was a sense of hostility amongst patients and pupils and midwives. There was an audible silence when I went over to do a ward round. In the end, God broke through my wall of hurt pride and I apologised for my unfair criticism, inferred from the tone of voice in the accusing question. Immediately, the tension eased and slowly relationships were restored and healed.

We were able to discuss the particular case quietly and impersonally to learn from it how to help one another better, should a similar situation recur. God was beginning to show me that this was part of "loving Him with all my heart", the willingness to accept heart burdens, and the will-ingness to break and apologise quickly for mistakes made or implied. "The sacrifice acceptable to God is a broken spirit; a broken and contrite heart, O God, Thou wilt not despise" (Psalm 51: 17). If to love equals to give, then I had to give

God my heart to break and to remould and to fill with His overflowing love. I wanted to, and yet I did not want to. I also wanted to retain the right to react and get angry, should I feel a situation warranted it. And God said: "No".

Something happened soon afterwards, that was to re-emphasise this lesson. I was to have gone to a distant forest village, for a missionary-mother's confinement: but I became ill, with a severe bout of malaria, complicated by jaundice. An African went the ninety-mile journey on a bicycle, with a letter from our missionary leader, explaining that I had been ill, but that I would come as soon as I was fit to travel, unless the family could make their way at once to our hospital at Nebobongo, where the mother could be given all the care she needed. This latter course would be preferable, as it would obviate the necessity of the long journey for me, so soon after being so unwell.

The cyclist returned in three days, with a letter for Jack Scholes. Their response was somewhat abrupt, written in apparent annoyance. They mentioned that their only vehicle was "off the road" waiting for a new universal joint. They practically demanded that I fulfil my promised obligations at once. The implication was that I was unaware of priorities, weighing my "trifling sickness" against the possibly serious consequences of a childbirth in the forest with no doctor or nurse present or available.

The news was conveyed to me tactfully and as kindly as possible. I agreed promptly that in a couple of days I would be fit enough to travel, despite slight residual fever and weakness, and so appropriate arrangements were made. Nevertheless, I was angry. I did not really stop to think about the cause of the reactions of that couple. Shut away in the forest, with no medical help and no available transport, they probably knew fear; much as my reaction when the baby died the previous month, and I knew frustration. It was their fear that had given rise to the abrupt letter, as my frustration had precipitated the angry question. Letter and question each carried an implied accusation of irresponsible negligence. The couple in the forest were thinking of themselves and their need: I at Nebobongo surrounded by patients had been thinking of myself and my involvement.

My leader knew me pretty well. He had been watching God's dealings in my life, and had heard my testimony as I sought to respond to this training. He came to see me and have a chat that evening, having discerned fairly accurately all that was going on in my heart.

"Helen," he said, "you need to learn that what God teaches you in your own circumstances about yourself, is to help you to understand others and to see things from their point of view."

He paused, and in my mind, I turned over what he had said.

"That couple are possibly afraid, away there on their own. It may not be easy for them to borrow transport, and it is a long rough journey, as you know well. For that young expectant mother it would be a tremendous ordeal. They have not realised how ill you have been, despite my letter to them. And we have to remember that they have been depending on you to see them through at this special time."

Of course all that he said was absolutely true, and quite easy to see and understand. But I was nursing my grievance, and my right to be hurt by their apparent selfishness.

"I want to ask you to do something – not for me, but for yourself," he said. "Actually, more truthfully, to do it for Christ's sake. As you go to-morrow, do all you can to help them. AND do not make too much of your illness. Jessie and I respect you for agreeing to go in these circumstances, as we know you are not really fit yet. God gave you the grace to make that decision. Now do not spoil it."

This was beyond me. What was he getting at?

"Just die to yourself, Helen, and the Lord will bless you," Jack continued. "You are going there to help them. Don't waste time justifying your delay, or underlining your virtue in going at all. You are going as Christ's servant. You'll only regret anything you say in haste or in anger: and most probably it would only be in self-defence or self-justification. Can you not trust God with all that? The Lord when He was reviled, reviled not in return . . . but He trusted to Him who judges rightly (I Pet. 2: 21–24). If you can accept that to these two your delay has caused distress and anxiety, God will help you to go to them in humility and to ask their forgiveness for it."

These new and searching thoughts chased through my mind. Somewhere deep down, a chord had been struck, and an echo was struggling up through my heart to try and find expression: but my rebellious anger sought to stifle it. Battle raged. I suppose I knew that he was right, but I did not want so high a standard. I wanted the right to blaze and proclaim my innocence of the implied accusation of irresponsible negligence.

And God said: "No."

God was teaching me, and I was slowly learning. That God did not always allow us to defend ourselves (or even each other, in certain circumstances) seemed very hard to me, particularly if one had clearly been wrongly accused or misjudged. Yet He reminded me that Christ, for my sake, was falsely accused at His trial and made no effort to defend Himself. "Like a sheep that before its shearers is dumb, so He opened not His mouth"(Is. 53: 7). Dimly I began to grope towards this higher goal. It was another step towards giving my heart wholly to God that He might love others through me, without my putting obstacles in His way: thus towards loving God with my whole heart.

* * *

Revival visited the church. The Holy Spirit was poured out on the local church. For years, senior missionaries and church pastors and faithful African women had been praying earnestly for such a visitation. They had started with one night each month given up to prayer. Then as prayer became more importunate, they added one day each month, set apart for prayer. As the sense of urgency grew, so a daily midday prayer meeting was held. Many spent hours in prayer and fasting on their own as well. God heard.

For ten days, a strange stirring had begun among the local workmen, and the Holy Spirit began a work of conviction in many hearts. Different ones confessed to thefts and returned stolen property. Others confessed to bitterness against white employers, and to jealousies regarding their possessions, and they sought forgiveness. Others again spoke of idleness, wasting their employer's time, discontent at working conditions: and they began working harder with a better spirit.

Then suddenly, on the Friday evening, at the weekly fellowship meeting, the Holy Spirit was poured out upon the one hundred folk gathered in the Bible School Hall. It was indeed a mighty, unforgettable awakening. Initially, there was a repercussion of shock and fear, as all over the hall, people were being shaken by the power of the Spirit, under the grip of conviction of sin, or else in a surge of irrepressible joy and release. Was this truly of God, or had some other spirit come amongst us?

As we heard the confessions of sin of those deeply convicted by the Spirit, and then how they claimed the shed blood of our Lord Jesus Christ for cleansing and forgiveness: as we saw their faces change and light up with a great inner joy, we knew the movement was truly of God. No other spirit would glorify the Lord Jesus, or convict men of sin, and lead them to the Cross for forgiveness. Men and women were under a deep constraint to see sin as very sinful, no longer making excuses for their "weaknesses and failures". Coldness of heart, petty jealousies, loss of temper, lack of desire for the things of God, impatience, irritability, all were called *sin* and confessed in order to be cleansed and forgiven.

Each individual entered into a new relationship with God. They became filled with joy. They sang. The singing was out of this world, filled with the joy of revival. Days and nights merged. Everything else was laid aside throughout that first weekend and the following week. God cleansed and revived His church. The joy was infectious, the singing vital and pulsating with life. There was a sense of abandonment in love for God. Some, of course, resisted: some remained outside, cynical and hard.

Prayer became the central pivot of the work of revival. Initially directed towards the needs of those of our own number who remained resistant and obdurate, slowly the burden changed, and a deep hunger grew for the salvation of the thousands around us. Witness teams began combing the surrounding villages, telling forth the Good News of Salvation. As they told others what God had done for them, and as their faces radiated their new-found joy and peace, hundreds came under conviction of sin, and were won to the Saviour. Hardened sceptics and amused scoffers alike were smitten down under the convicting power of the Spirit, unable to resist His compulsion. Many broke down in tears and wept their way to the Cross.

Throughout those days and weeks, the church appointed counsellors to be available at all hours to help those who were seriously seeking the way to be saved from the dominion of sin. These counsellors were deeply taught in the Word of God, and knew how to help those in spiritual need to find peace with God.

As a white-skinned missionary, I was automatically asked to be a counsellor. God knew how poorly prepared I was for such a role. I myself instinctively shrank from the task, knowing there were areas in my own life that I had not yet allowed God to deal with. How could I help others, when resisting help myself? I did not want to hear the stream of confessions as different ones unburdened their consciences, seeking forgiveness. I was afraid that I would be sullied by their sins, my mind polluted by listening to so much uncleanness. I steeled myself to hear with my outward ears only, to answer with the right words on my outward lips, but to garrison my heart from being hurt. In this process, I locked up my own sense of sin and failure, my own insecurity and lack of peace and assurance, determinedly resisting the work of the Holy Spirit in my own heart and life.

Three years passed by, years of intense activity. With an African team of co-workers, Florence Stebbing and I developed the medical centre at Nebobongo. We learned to make bricks, burn bricks, build bricks. We learned the intricacies of brick kilns, and measuring the cubic footage of felled trees for firewood, and filling in involved forms for legal permission to do each different job. We learned how a spirit level works, and the right mixture for cement and concrete, and how to simplify our complicated building plans to be a realistic project. We learned how to saw planks from a felled tree, over an open pit in the forest, using long two-handled saws: how to measure and raise these planks as triangular roof-trusses, to carry the corrugated asbestos sheeting: and by trial and error, how to mitre the corners of the latter to allow the short flanged nails to hold.

We learned motor mechanics. Not from choice, but sheer necessity, to keep at first a third-hand International van, and then a third-hand Chevrolet van on the road. We needed the vehicle to act as an ambulance, to bring patients to the hospital from out-lying districts: as builders' truck, to bring bricks from kiln to site, or asbestos sheeting from Isiro to Nebobongo: as food van, to collect the ton of plantains needed weekly by students and orphans, or to go to the annual markets of rice and of peanuts, to lay in stocks for the year. The only available text-book on car maintenance was in English (and unfortunately related to neither International nor Chevrolet) so the only way to do repairs was to get underneath or inside oneself, with an African colleague, and by trial and error, experiment till we succeeded.

We learned Swahili and French, and a smattering of Bangala and Kibudu: and then tackled the task of expressing medical truths without scientific jargon, in a manner simple enough to be understood, yet without distorting the essential truths. Both of us were keen on training nationals to do the work, Florence with a group of girls as pupil midwives, and myself with the fellows as student medical auxiliaries. There were plenty of problems. We had to learn to avoid making it all so easy that the students had no sense of responsibility, thinking they could do it all with no realisation of the dangers involved in a mistake: yet equally we had to learn to avoid making it so difficult that the pupils were discouraged, unable to grasp even the rudiments, and feeling they would never be of any use, developing a sense of inferiority towards our superior knowledge.

We wrote our first text-book in Swahili, checking facts and language with laborious effort in the late hours of each night when other work was over. Stencils were made, and eventually one hundred copies were duplicated on an old-fashioned machine where each page was meticulously rubbed off individually and laid out to dry. Agonised stories could be told of days when wind crept in through the shutters and lifted the pages in an avalanche of disaster!

We learned painfully how far we could and should transfer responsibility to the young shoulders of our African colleagues. They wanted so earnestly to "be as the white man" and yet they had no conception of what it meant to carry responsibility. So often we came head-on into disaster. After training one young male orderly to make up the routine mixtures used in the out-patients' clinic for coughs, for constipation, for diarrhoea and for malarial fever, the day came when we felt it was time to trust him without such close supervision as previously. All went well for a time. Then one sad day, all went wrong. It was about midday when I saw the first patient staggering towards the clinic, clutching his stomach, his face twisted in pain. I'd no idea what was wrong and could get no sense from him except: "Pain, pain, it hurts me with great bitterness!" Shortly afterwards, another patient was helped in, in like condition. Then a frightened mother came, carrying her screaming infant, thrashing about in her arms.

One of the students commented: "They were all three at this morning's clinic: how strange."

I pounced on it, and asked the student on duty to search out their treatment cards immediately. At a glance, I saw they had all received epsom salts. I grabbed the bottle of epsom salts and headed into the pharmacy.

"When did you make up this solution?"

"Last night. What is wrong?"

"Show me what you used – quickly."

The frightened orderly hesitated.

"What's wrong?" I cried. "You know there is something wrong with it?"

"Doctor, I'm sorry," he started to mumble.

"Never mind explanations now. Just show me what you used."

He produced a five-kilo brown-paper pack WITH NO LABEL, and pushed it to me. I opened it, smelled it, and then picking up one crystal, I licked it lightly. It was crude washing soda.

Eleven patients came back during the early afternoon. Fortunately a stomach wash-out, and a pint of milk to drink, with a raw egg beaten into it, made each feel better before nightfall.

What should be done? They had been told and told, until one was tired of repeating it, never to use an UN-LABELLED jar of medicine. It MUST be thrown out. Despite all our care, certain bottles invariably lost their labels through the efforts of cockroaches or of humidity or of much handling: and it was far safer to throw the contents away than to guess at their composition. All the students knew the rule. All the students knew the reasoning for the rule – or at least, they knew the reason the white lady gave for making the rule. But in the back of their minds there lingered the doubt as to its necessity. Was it just one more of these queer ideas of the foreigner? It was a shameful waste to throw out a new packet of an urgently needed medicine when it was so hard to get more, and when it was all so costly.

It needed a near-tragedy to prove the reason for the rule. Could we afford to learn by that method of trial and error when lives were at risk? Ought I to continue to supervise the making up of all medicines? But then how would they learn? How could I get over to them the reality and meaning of carrying responsibility?

A patient had come in with a severely slashed wrist. We repaired the damage under local anaesthesia with a tourniquet applied to the upper arm to control the haemorrhage. A student was left sitting by the patient afterwards, responsible for releasing the tourniquet every half-hour, and re-applying it if the haemorrhage recommenced. At nightfall, the student went off duty and another should have taken over. The latter failed to turn up, for some reason or other. The tourniquet was left on all night. I found it during the morning ward-round next day. The patient nearly lost his arm. Fortunately the tourniquet had worked itself just loose enough to allow a sufficient supply of blood through to keep the limb viable.

Who was responsible? They had been taught the rules. They had been carefully trained in the procedure of handing over responsibility from day to night staff. Should I have gone back to check? It was I who had applied the tourniquet in the first place. How would we know when we could trust them? If I went back every day to check every procedure, I should be considered "colonial" and unwilling to hand over to nationals the responsibility I had so far carried myself. At the risk of being misunderstood, and possibly even reported to a government official who was waiting for an excuse to accuse a white foreigner of an anti-national spirit, ought I not to continue to carry the final responsibility until they proved themselves capable?

A one-hundred bed hospital and maternity complex emerged from our building programme. A training school for national para-medical auxiliary workers was added, through our teaching efforts. A growing circle of dependent regional clinics and health centres was opened and staffed by graduates of the training school. Visits had to be made to each regularly for supervision, help, encouragement and provision of drugs. Still there was only one doctor and one qualified nurse at the centre. There was no off-duty time: each had to be on call day and night the whole year round. There was no qualified colleague with whom to share responsibility or with whom to discuss problems. The load seemed to grow heavier daily. Sick people from an enormous two-hundred-mile radius area made their way to us. There was no way out, no escape. There was no time to draw apart or assess the situation. And still it grew.

The day came when, on a medical ward-round in the hospital, I snapped at a woman patient. A small incident grew out of all proportion into a blazing row. Everyone in the ward became involved as they listened in horrified amazement to the Christian missionary doctor, as she lost her temper in fluent Swahili.

We left the ward and silently crossed the courtyard to the men's ward. Very graciously and humbly, John Mangadima spoke to me. He had been my first student, and had qualified two years before this incident. Since then, he and his wife had been to Bible School. He had now rejoined me at the hospital as my first medical assistant.

"Doctor," he said, "I don't think the Lord Jesus would have spoken like that."

I stood still, agonisingly still, my eyes shut, a great struggle in my weary heart. How right he was, how obviously right, and yet where did I go next? I wanted to break down and cry, to run away, to escape, to leave it all – but I could not.

We went back to the women's ward where I apologised.

I struggled on through a few more frustratingly irritating weeks. I knew God was speaking to me, but I would not listen. I wanted to listen, desperately so, and yet I would not. I deliberately closed my ears and hardened my heart. I piled up the excuses – my over-weariness, my taut nerves, the load of responsibility. But God was not listening to my well-reasoned arguments, and I was not listening to His still small voice of love.

Then one morning at our Bible study hour, I broke down. The Holy Spirit was working in the hearts of African students and pupils and workmen, but not in my cold, hard heart, and I could bear no more. The Lord "arranged" for Pastor Ndugu to be passing through Nebobongo that morning. He sized up the situation, made the necessary arrangements and invited me to accompany him to his village for a ten-day break. I followed him on my bicycle, haversack on back, the sixteen miles to his home. There he gave me a room, and left me alone.

I sought God's face for two unhappy days, but I could find no peace. The heavens seemed like brass and the Bible a closed book. Sunday evening, Pastor Ndugu called me out to the fireside where he and his wife, Tamoma, were sitting in the church hall. We prayed. A great still silence wrapped us around, only broken by the crackling firewood.

Gently he leaned towards me. "Helen," he said quietly and earnestly, "why can't you forget for a moment that you are white? You've helped so many Africans to find cleansing and filling and joy in the Holy Spirit through the blood of Jesus Christ. Why don't you let Him do for you what He has done for so many others?"

He went on, and opened up to me hidden areas in my heart that I had hardly even suspected, particularly this one of race prejudice. I was horrified. Could it really be true? I was out there to share with the nationals the Good News of the Gospel. I loved my African brethren. I cared . . . but did I? The Spirit forced me to acknowledge that subconsciously I did not really believe that an African could be as good a Christian as I was, or could know the Lord Jesus or understand the Bible as I did. My caring had in it an element of condescension, of superiority and of paternalism. Not that I had ever meant that it should: I just had not recognised the insidious effect of the whole colonial system and my own acceptance of it as the necessary basis of our work.

I began to confess: the Spirit continued to reveal and break. Hidden envies and jealousies towards other missionaries; resentments over certain treatments and committee decisions; fear at the frustration caused by insufficient training to carry the responsibility; unloading this frustration on to colleagues by impatient irritation; criticism of others and pride in my own achievements. There were many apologies needed, restitutions to be made, forgiveness to be sought from family and fellowship.

Then the Lord reminded me of my attitude as a counsellor during the days of revival, how I had been unwilling to be sullied, fearful of being hurt by their sins. God spoke to me:

"I was not only sullied by your sin in order to redeem you: I became your sin, that you might become My righteousness" (II Cor. 5: 21).

The sheer wonder of the greatness of His sacrifice for me broke my heart afresh. He so loved ME that He gave Himself for ME. He was MY ransom. He bore MY sins and iniquities, and with His stripes I was healed. And He was inviting me to identify with Him and with the Africans among whom He had placed me as His witness. If I were willing to let Him whittle away the protective bark – this ability to withdraw or to become impersonal so as not to be hurt by, or finally involved in, a situation – He would bring me into a new oneness with Himself and with others.

"That they may all be one; even as Thou, Father, art in Me, and I in Thee, that they also may be in us: ... that they may be one even as we are one, I in them and Thou in Me, that they may become perfectly one ..." (John 17: 21–23).

God seemed to say to me: "Oh, yes, you will be hurt, sullied, entering right into heart unity on the level of each individual's need, and so be able to share, to feel, to yearn with others in that need, and together seek cleansing and forgiveness. Yes, it will cost – in time and involvement. Your heart may often be crushed: very possibly some will try to take advantage of you, others will misunderstand you. It can easily lead to false accusations, misconstruction of motives, even deeper pain. But it is My way, the way of the Cross. Do you want it?"

And I did: with all my heart I wanted it, and I asked God to continue the whittling process.

As I cycled back to Nebobongo early the following Monday morning, I was churning over in my mind just how I would share with our African church fellowship all I had learned that week. Reaching home, I was unexpectedly met by a small welcome committee! One took my bicycle, another the haversack. Before I could say anything, John Mangadima burst out:

"Oh, Doctor, hallelujah!"

Startled, I looked at him. I hadn't said a thing.

"Oh," he laughed, "You don't need to tell us, your face tells us. We've been praying for you for four years!"

And I had gone out to them as the missionary-teacher!

The first major "'cost" that I encountered in seeking to love God with all my heart was in the giving up of my pride – pride of nationality, pride of education, pride of natural abilities. God has continually to break me on each of these. They get in the way of love, real outgoing love. Then He has to deal with my self – self-reliance, self-justification, self-pity. These too hinder the free flow of His love. Step by step, as God deals with pride and the insidious love of self, He can take my heart and truly love others through it.

To love God with all my heart is to give Him my heart, that He may fill it and overflow it with His own self-giving love for all among whom He sends me to live.

## Chapter 2

# With ALL my soul

*Father, if Thou art willing, remove this cup from me; nevertheless not my will, but Thine, be done.*

LUKE 22: 42

DURING MY MONTHS at our missionary training centre, I was well taught to "count the cost" before signing on the dotted line to be a willing member of the fellowship prepared to obey its rules. In attempting to define the cost, it was made clear that among other things it involved the possibility (if not the definite probability) of leaving home and loved ones, of remaining single, of leaving my job and in consequence the security of a settled salary and future pension. We were taught to rely on God, as our faithful Master, responsible for the supply of all our needs, as He has promised: "My God will supply every need of yours according to His riches in glory in Christ Jesus" (Phil. 4: 19). Should one marry, God would be equally responsible for the partner and for any children, their safety and their education. We would leave the comparative security of our home system of justice. There would be problems of communications in another country – not merely because of an at-present unknown language, but also, when known, in gaining facility in the idiomatic use of that language – and such difficulty could lead to loneliness and a sense of isolation and misunderstanding. There might well be long hours of thankless toil at a job for which one was not really trained (such as a medical doctor having to make a brick kiln in order to build a hospital!).

I listened and thought I understood what was meant – at least vaguely! I accepted the prospect of difficulties easily and willingly, so keen was I to be fully involved in the privileged role of "being a missionary". I could think of no more wonderful vocation than being an ambassador of the Lord Jesus Christ, His representative to a people in need. I was called to Congo/Zaire through a phrase in Isaiah 58: 12, "You shall be called the repairer of the breach," going out to be the first missionary doctor in that area, to fill a gap in the church ministry by providing a medical service. I was thrilled and excited. Nothing could discourage me then. I had no real interest in clothing and possessions, money or position. I had very little sense of giving anything up: it was all a sense of gain, in the privilege of serving where one was needed. I day-dreamed big castles in the air!

Over the first four years, I gathered together a few personal possessions as everyone does: my home at Nebobongo began to fill up with pictures on the walls (photos from calendars, cellophaned to cardboard), rush mats on the floors, and books on the shelves. Rough wooden planks balanced on bricks, those shelves were not very ornate, but the books they held became increasingly precious. There was a growing library of Bible commentaries and devotional books, including some fairly rare copies of thirteenth and fourteenth century mystics. There were much used medical and surgical text-books, kept up to date by the generosity of family and medical friends, with all the monthly *Practitioner* journals. There were some highly prized, personally signed first edition books, collected for me by those who were in the book-lovers' world. All the books were shellac-sprayed to keep off cockroaches. They were regularly dusted and rubbed over, to keep off the damp-mould of the humid climate. They were loved.

The home I lived in had been built some thirteen years

previously by another missionary; the building had a high-pitched, grass-thatched roof. White ants had invaded this, despite all our watchful precautions, and the endless repairs required had eventually driven us to decide to replace the thatch with permanent corrugated asbestos sheeting. The material was acquired and stored. When the dry season was well established, with the promise of at least five weeks without a drop of rain, we stripped off the old grass roof. The high pitched beams were measured, marked, sawn and lowered with great care on make-shift pulleys into their new positions. All was in readiness to put on the new roof tomorrow.

I went to bed that night under the stars, gazing up at the bare rafters and through to the dark arch of the sky. Suddenly I was awakened, startled, What had wakened me? Searching round in the dark for my torch, I realised that I was wet. Then I heard the steady swishing sound. I cast the narrow beam of light around the four walls of my bedroom, through the cascading rain, to see the crumpled "pictures" drooping from the walls which were being rapidly denuded of their white lime-wash. The floor was awash with a mixture of mud and lime. The bed was soaking. I crawled out, and flung my raincoat over the pillow and upper end, still partially dry from where I had been lying and from the protection of the mosquito netting. I collected an umbrella, but was too disheartened to do more. What was there to do, anyway? I crept back into bed, sitting cross-legged on the pillow, with the umbrella over my head, an open Bible on my knees, a torch in my hand, amid the continuing destruction of my possessions – and I wept.

"... joyfully accepting the plundering of your property ..."

The words from a verse in Hebrews mocked me. The steady patter of rapidly falling rain, the rising moan of the wind in the trees outside, the dark sky above torn with vivid forks of lightning, all seemed to mock me. It was the dry season. It never rained.

We had not moved pictures or mats or books because it never rained during the six weeks from Christmas until early February. By morning, there was over an inch of water throughout the house, unable to escape because of the sills at the doors which were there to prevent the storms coming *in*. Everything was soaked, and caked with mud and lime.

I could not bear to look at the books.

It was thirty-six hours before the sun returned; two days before others could finish sweeping out the house, drying out the mats and mopping the books. Then we began the painstaking process of dabbing each page dry separately. The shellac made them sticky. The pages were endless. And every day, all the ordinary work had to be done as well – ward rounds, student lectures, emergency surgery, special clinics – so the page-dabbing had to be relegated to the lonely night hours when others had gone to bed. And self-pity reared its head again.

"Do you love Me, more than these?" a voice asked me.

In its setting, asking me if I still thought I loved the Lord more than my fellow-missionaries or African colleagues did: or taken out of context as the Spirit applied it to my own immediate circumstance, asking me if I still loved my Lord more than my precious books: the phrase challenged me to be real. Was my love a pretence? If I really loved God as deeply and keenly as I professed, how could I be so upset over the spoiling of my books, a few material possessions? Had God, perhaps, allowed this to occur to make me face reality?

I had gone out to Africa so enthusiastically, certain there was no cost that I was unwilling to pay for the privilege of serving God and of being one of His missionaries. In a few years, my values had shifted. When I first arrived at Ibambi, my whole life was giving up to serving the people, seeking to reveal the love of God to them. And I had been somewhat critical of others who I considered had lesser ideals. I had been sure that only 100 per cent devotion to God was good enough, and even that would still only leave us as "unprofitable servants" simply doing our duty. Now I had slipped into the rut of enjoying putting a small home together, and gathering round me a few pretty things, and making life a little easier.

There was nothing wrong with having pictures on the walls, mats on the floors, or books on the shelves, so long as they were not important in my life. If they began to take the place of my "first love", they would have to go. To love the Lord my God with all my emotions and feelings and desires was going to demand a stiff standard of discipline, a firm deliberate sorting out of priorities. To become an arrow in His hands, the leaves and attractive blossoms would have to go.

I did not learn the lesson over-night, but I did start to re-evaluate my priorities. I was fearful of allowing anything to lessen my love for God. There were many other "soulish" influences that came in, however. I began to want pretty clothes, but was largely dressed from the second-hand clothes that came for the Africans. I received sacks of these from the post-office, and unpacked them, so I had first choice. I would go through them the night they came, and choose the dress that fitted me best, in good condition, and the colour I preferred. The rest of the sack would be distributed in the village the next day.

It seems a small thing now, as I look back: yet was it fair? The clothes were actually sent for the Africans. Why did I consider that I had the right to pick the best first, before others even saw them?

The Lord convicted me about my spirit in this little affair. I remember a choking feeling of self-pity. "Is even this wrong, Lord? All I want is something a little brighter and newer and better fitting. I don't want anything expensive or fashionable." But I did want first choice! – and I didn't want others to know that it had come out of the sack. I didn't want them to know that I was too poor to buy myself a new dress, and too ignorant to make one. I expect I was ashamed somehow. Others had stronger or better faith, and received what they needed without resort to stealing from gifts sent to the Africans.

That thought did it. I sneaked the dress concerned back into the supply, and saw someone else's eyes light up with joy as she tried it on and pirouetted before the other women. God, of course, provided what I needed by other means! He was only trying to teach me a principle, removing another leaf that was unnecessary for His arrow. He wanted my single-eyed affection, my whole-hearted love.

Another small incident in this long process of training comes vividly to my remembrance. It will seem unbelievable in our Western affluent society, yet the principle, if not the detail, remains the same. One month I had travelled the fifty miles north to Isiro in our Mission truck to shop for everyone. The day before, I had collected from each family lists of what was needed. The trip was being combined with taking a missionary to the airport, for her flight home to England on furlough. After seeing her off, I went into the town to tackle the shopping.

I finished the day at a greengrocer's, where all the fresh vegetables were on one central stall in multiple compartments. A large notice stated that they were all at "17f/kg", about 3s/lb. in 1957 English terms. I counted out how much money I had left, and then selected vegetables for each family in turn, as I thought they would like them.

As I walked round, looking and feeling and choosing, I suddenly saw bright red, large, delicious looking APPLES. I hadn't seen an apple for five years! I weighed out one kilo, some eight apples, and added them to the growing pile in my basket.

Eventually I took all to the counter; the assistant reweighed and counted everything, scribbling the price on each packet, and totalling all, she passed me the bill. It was larger than I had expected, but I had just enough to pay. I left the shop, and then decided to check why it was so much more than I had calculated. The apples were marked 70f/kg, rather than the 17f/kg of everything else! 1s. 6d. of 1957 English money for each apple – or in 1970's values, it might be 75p each.

Horrified, I turned to take them back. Three things met me. First, the door was locked. It was 5 p.m. and they had closed. Secondly, I saw a large notice which said clearly and unmistakably "Fresh apples arrived to-day at 70f/kg": and, thirdly, a small notice which stated concisely and unequivocally "After leaving the store, no goods can be returned or exchanged."

More than 5p a bite! My heart sank. What foolish thing had I done, in a thoughtless moment of self-indulgence? We could have bought two bottles of pencillin with that money, enough to treat four patients with broncho–pneumonia. Would I never learn to curb my impetuous extravagant nature?

Then self-pity reared its head! "Surely and why not? Why shouldn't you enjoy a pound of apples? Those friends at home who sent you money this month will be thrilled to know you've used a little for yourself and not put it all in the hospital. You know they underlined that it was to be a PERSONAL gift."

This argument did not help to change my honest appraisal that the action I had taken was not the highest in God's eyes, however easily it could be justified to anyone else. To love the Lord my God with all my soul would have to mean that He controlled my desires, and took over my impetuous nature, and replaced my self-centredness with His own self-giving nature.

Books, clothes, food. What else was He going to touch? Where else was I failing Him, failing to love Him with all my soul, my emotions and my will? When I went home on my first furlough there was an unexpected opportunity to marry. Through the first five years in Africa, I had never really given it much thought. I was busy, more than busy, and could not be bothered to think about "what might have been". I liked living alone, and being free to get things done. But one thought had become alarmingly large. I dreaded the realisation that I would have to accept the responsibility to do surgery.

During my fifth year in Africa, our second missionary doctor had joined me at Nebobongo, after four years' service elsewhere in our area in Congo/Zaire. He came to Nebobongo very much at my suggestion, to train me in surgery, so that, after my furlough in my second term of service, I could go south to Mulito to open a new medical centre there. Many thousands of people in the south were in great need of medical and surgical care. The responsibility in surgery involves not only the skill and knowledge needed to do the actual operation, but also the wisdom to be able to decide on whom to operate and when. All this frightened me. If I were married to a missionary surgeon, the problem would be solved.

It was very selfish reasoning. I also realised it would be nice to have a man around to mend things in the house or under the car! It would be good to have a companion with whom to share both joys and problems. But I did not honestly want a husband for any deeper level of emotional need. Just that he'd be useful. Maybe this seems very materialistic and pragmatic: certainly it was selfish.

During my furlough, I arranged to do a year of medical practice, six months in general medicine, six months in general surgery, in two British hospitals, as refresher courses. I needed to learn all I could in order to give a better service in Africa. This was a splendid opportunity to look for the "ideal" husband, a Christian surgeon, called to missionary service, with the Worldwide Evangelization Crusade, in Congo/Zaire, willing to be my husband.

Such do not grow on trees!

Before the year was out, so strongly had I set my emotions in one direction that I asked WEC for a year's leave of absence. Being a missionary with WEC was an obvious obstacle to getting married. All the priorities went. Loving God, serving as a missionary, my responsibility to my African colleagues and friends, all became secondary to my pursuit of a husband. God let me go. He did not force me to conform to His pattern for my life. He allowed me to exercise my free will, however deeply I grieved Him in doing so.

Disillusionment followed. Honest sorrow that I had so deeply grieved God, saddened the Mission, failed my colleagues. I punished myself, as I thought, harshly and relentlessly. I worked out my year of leave of absence from WEC, and then asked if I might return with them to Congo. I was interviewed: papers were filled in: letters were written. Eventually it was agreed I might return.

Yet I went back with an unresolved problem and a resultant deep reservation. I had rejected God's love in my impatient chase of what I wanted. I had deliberately chosen not to love Him first, nor with my whole soul. And I knew I had done this, with my eyes open. It seemed too easy just to come to Him for forgiveness. My "feelings" took over and directed my reasoning. I *felt* that I did not deserve an easy forgiveness. I had known what I was doing, and acted wilfully and deliberately. I *felt* I had to pay a price, and prove the reality of my sorrow and repentance. I *felt* I had no right to seek, or ask for, or expect any relationship with God during this period. I chose to shut the "door" into God's presence, and to remain outside. So for four years, I lived in Africa as a missionary, doing the right things, saying the right things, giving to others the appearance of "being a good missionary". I taught daily in church. I loved those teaching sessions. I believed utterly in the Bible, and our need of Biblical Truth to guide us daily. I never doubted that the ONLY way of salvation and sanctification was through and in our Lord Jesus Christ.

I taught others, yet I found no peace for my own tortured heart. I would not allow myself to believe there was still hope for me. Though it was the Truth and the only Truth, I had sacrificed my right to its blessing by my own wilful behaviour and disobedience to His commandments.

"Sacrificed my right to ..." I have no rights. I have no right to *feel* saved, to *feel* at peace. I have no right to work out my own salvation in the way I choose. I had never deserved to be forgiven in the first place when I was converted. I could do nothing to merit God's favour, His grace, His love. If all I had ever known was unmerited and undeserved Grace, how could I then forfeit that which I had never earned?

"Lest having preached to others, I myself should be disqualified (or become a castaway)" (I Cor. 9: 27).

Two voices in my heart called in opposite directions, and my dependence on my feelings obstructed my hearing God's voice of love. Even through the Bible teaching that I gave to others, I knew that having confessed what had been wrong, by His Grace, through the merits of Christ's one perfect sufficient sacrifice, I was forgiven. Yet was I? Doubts gnawed at my assurance. I could not find peace in my heart to accept His proffered forgiveness. I knew I did not deserve it ... but I never had deserved it ... and so the round of argument, of feelings, of doubt, started again.

Was I too proud, in some strange inverted way, to humble myself to accept an unmerited forgiveness? Knowing it was all of Grace, yet my inner being wanted the right to do something to merit it. I was trying to work out my own salvation, to earn God's forgiveness, to prove the sincerity of my repentance.

Then the civil uprising came, and I, along with many others, was taken captive by rebel soldiers. They stole our possessions: they invaded our privacies. They were brutal and cruel as they humiliated us and insulted us. In the midst of the suffering, at last, I allowed myself to hear God's clear voice.

"For what credit is it, if when you do wrong and are beaten for it, you take it patiently? but if when you do right and suffer for it, you take it patiently, you have God's approval (this is acceptable with God)" (I Peter 2: 20).

God, in His immeasurable Grace, said to me yet again: "Now will you accept what I have been offering you all these years? I love you. I have forgiven you. I want you to enjoy My love and the job I want to do through you."

At last I knew that it was true. It was not based on my feelings or on my emotions. It was not dependent on my faith or my obedience. In no way could I merit or deserve it. He loved me. He knew me through and through, better than I knew myself, and yet still, He loved me. Christ died on Calvary to tell me that. Christ lives in heaven, an unceasing intercessor on my behalf to make that love real to me in my experience.

It was an unforgettable experience. God was so vitally real, so totally understanding. His comfort was so complete, so entirely without condemnation. I really knew that His love was unutterably sufficient. His love was wholly able to meet my deepest need: He was not even judging me for my unwillingness to believe and accept His love through the previous years. A great peace took possession of my whole being, not just a peace in my feelings, but a tangible fact of peace even apart from feelings, even in the midst of physical fear and suffering.

As He began to take control of my emotions, I began to realise the truth of Phil. 4: 19: "and my God will supply every need of yours according to His riches in glory in Christ Jesus". It was true on all levels, not just for financial issues, nor yet only for spiritual mysteries on an exalted plane, but also for everyday, down-to-earth emotional needs of soul and body. As I began to move out of "feelings" and on to "facts", I realised that He was satisfying me, not only with an inner assurance of salvation and forgiveness, but also with a reality of love and depth of companionship that actually took from me, at that time, any sense of need or loneliness. Christ was truly becoming my "sufficiency": I was learning to love Him with all my soul.

Yet still the lesson was not learnt. I become so easily emotionally involved with and for those among whom I work. Every death in the hospital upset me. To be awakened at three a.m. by the death-wail is a sad experience. After going over to the ward, doing what I could to calm the family and to comfort the bereaved, I would take the patient's notes and go back home to look over them again and again in detail. Had we failed to do anything that we could have done? Had I anticipated the problem, and expected the outcome, or had I been at fault in my diagnosis? I never learnt to "accept death philosophically"; I never became accustomed to the death-wail, even though the majority of our patients arrived in an advanced stage of their illness, often having already tried the skills of the witch-doctor, and were therefore inevitably more moribund than an equivalent percentage of patients in any hospital in Britain.

Another realm of emotional involvement was the student body. Our training school accepted between twelve to twenty-four eighteen-year-old lads every year, to give them two years of training to become practical nurses. Many came from distant villages, representing many tribes and different languages. They arrived often fearful and insecure, never before having left their own tribal area. Overnight they became my spiritual sons. I loved them and cared for them. I gave all I had to train them, not only medically, but as young men to serve the Lord and to serve their own people, as medical evangelists.

Then something would happen. A promising second year student was brought before the church elders for discipline, and I would break my heart. Jason, the evangelist's son, was accused of adultery with the wife of a tuberculosis patient. It was later proved to be a false accusation, but he was disciplined for a year, and my heart ached for him and for his parents. Michael was involved in a murder case in a local village. He was thrown into prison after narrowly escaping with his life from the fury of the family. This too proved false, but in bitterness, he turned from God and went far away from us into a life of sin. Our hearts felt crushed. Robert, a fine senior student, nearing his finals, was found to be drinking heavily and to be involved in many practices contrary to church and school rules. He would not admit his fault, and reluctantly, with heavy hearts, we dismissed him. Bernard, a graduate working on the staff of the school, fell to the temptation of stealing drugs and selling them on the

black market. Accused by his wife, he flew into an awful
rage and attacked her with a long knife: and would have
burned their thatch cottage to the ground, soused in petrol,
had the alarm not been raised in time to prevent further
tragedy. He would not let us help him. Dismissed and dis-
graced, he divorced his wife, rejected his young sons, took
another wife, and went to live and work in the city, publicly
rejecting all Christian fellowship.*

Again and again, my heart cried out under the burdens, as
I carried their shame and their sorrow, as I grieved over
their hardness of heart and unwillingness to repent. I
pleaded with each one. I spent hours with them, talking of
God's love and grace, patience and forbearance. I knew
what I was talking about: had I not experienced it? As ultimately in each of these cases, I had to fill in the official
"document of discipline", sending copies to the Government stating why each student had been dismissed from the
school and would not therefore be presented for the final
examinations for which their names were already entered, I
felt like a mother spurning her own son, turning him out of
home, knowing he had nowhere else to go.

The emotional involvement of my aroused feelings had to
be taken again and again to the Saviour. I had to learn that
He cared for the students even more than I did. He demanded a holy church, and His will for each member was
sanctification. I dared not lower the standards to accommo-
date one individual, or the whole would suffer. God invited
me to give Him this part of my make-up, to love Him with
all my soul, and to trust Him to work out His infinite purposes in His infinite love, even without my understanding.

Books – clothes – food – companionship – death –

* The names of most Africans have been changed to hide identities.
In some cases, place names have also been changed when this seemed
wise, but the stories are all true.

C

discipline – all involved "feelings". There seemed so much to learn in this realm, in order to love Him with all my feelings: yet this was only one part of my soul. The other, and perhaps, larger and stronger part, was my WILL. If I would learn to love God with all my soul, I would have to learn to give Him my will. That would mean giving Him the right to exercise control over it. I had to learn that I have no rights. All rights are His. How was I ever going to learn to live in the atmosphere of the prayer: "Not my will, but Thine, be done"?

My right to be considered, to have my opinion listened to, to give my advice, to make choices and decisions, certainly in so far as these related directly to my own life and the outworking of the vision He had given me, all seemed so essentially right and reasonable. It is against all modern teaching and practice to deny any human being the right to be themselves and to express themselves. Hence the freedom of speech, and of the press, and many other avenues of self-expression have become precious and almost fundamental to our whole way of life and thinking. Psychologically it is sound. Intellectually it is reasonable. Practically, it may lead to anarchy and strikes and disruption of whole communities, though perhaps one might not say so (even in these days of freedom of speech!). This is considered a small price to pay for a basic freedom.

However, spiritually, it is not God's way. He has a perfect plan for each one of us, that fits in to His over-all purpose for the whole world. My individual liberty is safeguarded within His plan, in so far as I am free to choose to accept or reject it: but once I have accepted it, I must give obedience to Him within it, and learn to say wholeheartedly: "Not my will, but Thine, be done." If I truly believe in Him, I'll trust Him to desire for me that which is for my highest good, and to have planned for its fulfilment.

How hardly this comes! When the committee of senior missionaries, responsible for the over-all planning of church ministries in our area of Congo/Zaire, decided to ask me to go to Nebobongo to set up the medical centre there, I was furious. There was no medical worker on the committee and I felt at least I should have had the right to explain why, to me, this was a very bad decision. No rights! As the work developed at Nebobongo over the years, we have never ceased to see all the difficulties and disadvantages involved in that original decision, and yet God has abundantly vindicated His plan and fulfilled His purpose.

When the committee decided that I should go on furlough in July 1958, after only five years of service, I was indignant. Why couldn't I do seven years – or more – as everyone else? At least, I had the right to be consulted. Would it be convenient to my Mother and family for me to go then? No rights. Another doctor and I had arrived in Congo the same year, 1953. One had to go on the first furlough and return to cover for the other. There were reasons (not explained to me) why it seemed best that I should go first. God was in control and it was in His plan. The future proved how exactly right the decision and timing had been.

Years later, a certain wealthy American businessman wanted to help and encourage us in the reconstruction of the medical services in north-eastern Zaire, following the unbelievable destruction of the rebellion. Various suggestions were made as to how this aid could be best employed. It is often not easy for the one who makes a gift to understand the reasoning and decision of the recipient who is living in conditions and a culture so different from his own. One suggestion had emerged with regard to setting up a "clothing factory", training and equipping national workers to make uniforms necessary for the medical personnel. Even though the details for developing the suggestion were over-optimistic, nevertheless I felt that it could be adapted to meet a need of our people, and to reduce costs for an essential commodity.

I was willing to accept responsibility and to train a group of nationals to take it over. The committee refused permission. Doubtless they could foresee all the snags and involvements, such as the possibility of strikes and demands for unrealistic pay rises, and we had enough troubles without creating more. Also, clearly, it could not be considered a priority, in the midst of urgent needs for better surgical and medical facilities and equipment. I attempted to compromise and run a "mini" factory: that is, a one-roomed tailor shop with two sewing machines and two men to operate them. This was partly in order that the donor should not be offended by our refusal to accept his generosity in the way he wished to express it. Surely I had the right to do that. No-one else would be involved. There would be no commercial aspect as it would be limited strictly to a service for our own employees only.

No rights. God had to teach me over and over again. It seemed I would not, or could not, understand what He was saying. This particular "small" affair snow-balled, and accusation and counter-accusation were thrown from one to another, till many were hurt, and much unnecessary offence was given. The work closed down. No more was said. Yet certain souls, bruised through misunderstandings and false accusations, took many years to heal. If only I had given in to God's right to rule and direct my will, much of that need never have occurred.

Perhaps most vividly this fight over my right to exercise my will in deciding issues and directing policies, came to a head in my last year at Nyankunde. The story of that traumatic year, (including the death of my senior missionary, Jack Scholes: several long truck journeys over the three hundred and fifty rough miles to and from Nebobongo and Ibambi, and Nyankunde: repeated attempts to finalise government recognition of our WEC medical service, and of the CME training school for medical auxiliaries: the revolt of the third year girl students against learning midwifery: the school inspection: the preparation for handing over all departments of my work to my successors: and finally the student strike) has been told in some detail in another place.*

I had been in Africa twenty years, and felt fairly confident in dealing with most situations, especially those regarding personnel. I prided myself on maintaining a good student/staff relationship: and yet that last year everything went wrong. Despite every approach to the third year girl students, we never won their confidence, and they forced us, against our will, to do what they wanted. I was ill during the year, and in order to make up to the students for all the lectures they missed, we offered to change the programme, certainly to the staff's disadvantage. The third year students refused en bloc to accept the change, unless we paid them extra for any resultant over-time on practical duties. A girl, dismissed for repeated trouble-making, stirred up her father to bring a case against me in the courts, charging me with "anti-party subversive techniques", a charge that could cause my Government dossier to be so marked that I would never be allowed to return to the country. This charge cost me three months of a long drawn out court case, and much unpleasant publicity, with the continual threat of imprisonment or expulsion.

Then finally the student body went on strike. It was the last Monday of the school year. Final exams were over. Summer holidays were starting within a week. And the simmering pot of resentments boiled over. It was the last chance

* *He Gave Us a Valley* by Helen Roseveare, published by IVP in 1976.

for that group of third year students. A week earlier, would
have jeopardised their chances of gaining the coveted
government diploma. A week later, many would have been
on holiday and the impact would have been greatly dim-
inished. It was cleverly timed. It was cleverly planned.

I was very tired at the end of that year. I was quite unpre-
pared for what occurred. I was deeply immersed in my own
problems, of dealing with government return sheets, student
holiday arrangements and travel vouchers, and concluding
arrangements for handing over to my successors in six
weeks' time.

I was totally unable to cope with the strike. The school
committee had to call in higher authority to sort out the
tangled mess of broken relationships. The college students
openly defied me, charging me with corrupt management of
school affairs. The staff, national and foreign, were afraid
that my method of approach was inflaming the trouble and
widening the breach. The executive committee of hospital
management decided that I had been inflexible and unable
to see another's point of view. I was annoyed and hurt. Had
I no right, as college principal, to be trusted, my word believed? Did I really have to justify myself in a common
court against the lying accusations of a group of unruly students?

No rights. The committee asked me to re-consider my
decision. I felt that any change of judgment with regard to
the matter basic to the disagreement could only be a
compromise of principle, so I refused. Had I no right at least
to maintain my own code of ethics? Apparently not. The
only way out of the impasse was my resignation, which was
regretfully accepted, allowing the management to re-nego-
tiate with the students, particularly with regard to the use of
their scholarship money: and to reach an agreement acceptable to both.

It was a sad end to twenty years of hard work. The college had finally achieved government recognition. The teaching material was well prepared and the courses all established. It could have been a success story, the building programme nearing completion and a well-organised graduation day planned as my final farewell. Instead, it had all gone wrong. What was God saying to me?

I had prayed so often: "Not my will, but Thine, be done," and I had seriously endeavoured to enter in the spirit of "no rights". Unwittingly I had retained the right to think of the college as "my" college, the students as mine, the government recognition as my success story. God had often shown me that I was to have no rights, no right to decide or to choose, no right to own or to possess. All rights were to be His. If I gave Him my will honestly (which I believe for me is the ultimate meaning of loving God with all my soul) then He alone had the right to control and guide my will. I become a vessel to contain Him, a temple in which He dwells and from which He directs His affairs. Yet I had tried to retain the right to consider it "my" work. Then, as I would not give it up voluntarily, He found a means to constrain me to give it up, even against my will. It hurt: of course it hurt. For a moment I felt so hurt and rebellious that I considered the "cost" too much to pay. Yet I had told the Lord that I truly wanted to love Him with all my soul, and that therefore I wanted Him to take my will and my emotions and to transform them into His image to work out His purposes.

So the whittling process of transforming a branch to an arrow continues. The love of books and pretty possessions was like the flowers and the leaves, being torn off. The sin of unbelief and the reliance on my feelings were the thorns and knots that damaged the balance of the arrow, and so had to go. The desire for my rights, so as to preserve my own personality, had to be stripped off, as the bark, if I were to become truly usable in His purposes.

"Lord, grant me Thy Grace to go on praying: 'Not my will, but Thine, be done.' "

## Chapter 3

# With ALL my mind

*My thoughts are not your thoughts, neither are your ways my ways, says the Lord. For as the heavens are higher than the earth, so are my ways higher than your ways, and my thoughts than your thoughts.*

ISAIAH 55: 8, 9

I WAS DETERMINED from the start to be a good doctor, and to give to the local people the best possible medical service. I hated the thought that "anything is better than nothing" if that were going to undermine standards. Surely there could be nothing wrong with such an ambition? Yet it proved to be a leaf on the branch, which had to be pruned off in the process of making the arrow.

One morning I was down at the brick kiln, helping to organise a team to empty the kiln and transport the 20,000 bricks to the building site as speedily as possible, with the minimum of breakages. My hands were rough and torn, as I was unaccustomed to such work. A pupil midwife came to call me to see a patient in the maternity section of the hospital. Examining the woman, I knew that if I operated at once I could possibly save the mother and baby alive. I began to scrub up: my hands smarted under the bristles. I held out my hands to the nurse to pour on antiseptic alcohol: I drew in my breath sharply at the stinging pain. And in my mind, a small voice of complaint started.

Why had not God arranged for another missionary, preferably a man, to be appointed to Nebobongo to see to the buildings and all that side of the work, so that I could be free to give the people the best medical care of which I was capable? So much of my time was occupied with buildings: in weekly visits to local markets to bargain for our needed food supplies: in the repair and upkeep of our vehicles: in supervision of the primary school and orphanage. There was hardly time to prepare adequately for the lectures for the student auxiliary nurses, even when there were no emergency calls. A run of these, plus several disturbed nights, and the whole programme was disrupted.

The following Wednesday evening, I mentioned all this to the church council and asked their prayers, that I might not become resentful. One godly man, after leading the group in believing prayer, smiled at me and offered a kindly rebuke.

"Doctor," he said, "when you are being a doctor, in your white coat, stethoscope round your neck, speaking French, you are miles from us. We fear you and all say: 'Yes, yes,' hardly even hearing what you said. But when you are down at the kiln with us, and your hands are rough as ours are: when you are out at the markets, using our language and making howlers and we all laugh at you: that's when we love you, and how we have come to trust you and can listen to what you tell us of God and His ways."

I felt humbled and accepted from God that even rough hands were worth that. It wasn't the way that I had pictured it or expected it to be, but I could see that God knew best.

A year later, my complaint was reversed. The hospital was built and functioning, and the news had gone round a large region that there was a doctor at Nebobongo who could do operations and whose drugs were powerful. In particular the news spread that if women had their babies at Nebobongo, they would live. When the work was first started, it was not unusual for a mother at the ante-natal clinic to say that she had had ten or twelve or even fifteen children born to her but that only two or three were now living. Now a change was coming as we brought hygiene and loving care and obstetric knowledge to their service.

And patients began streaming in, day and night, some coming as much as three hundred miles to us. I had no time for anything but medicine, medicine, medicine. Always there were patients, queueing up, waiting hopefully. Always there were empty medicine bottles waiting for carefully weighed and measured contents. Always there were specimens on the table in the laboratory, waiting to be examined. Medicine, medicine, medicine. There was no let up. There was hardly time for meals or sleep. There was no off-duty. I had hoped to be a good misionary, to be able to preach the Gospel to out-patients, to sit by bedsides in the wards and tell the good news of salvation. But there was time for nothing but medicine.

One night, I had been up non-stop for forty-eight hours. It was after one in the morning, as I was leaving the operating theatre. Pulling off my gloves in a basin of water, desperately tired, I began to grumble inwardly. It was all becoming unreasonable. There was no way out of it. I knew that I just could not keep going much longer if the pressures did not let up. Surely God could see that. Could He not send someone to help us, to relieve us? – not that I had any idea as to whom, but surely God could do something.

"Doctor," – a nurse came in, hesitantly, almost apologetically, knowing how tired I must be. "There are two patients lying on the verandah. They were carried in from Opienge a short while ago."

Opienge! That was over two hundred miles away. I went out and examined them. One was a young catechist in his early thirties. He had a strangulated hernia. He was in a bad condition. I reckoned that if we operated at once, there was just a chance that we could save his life: if we left him till the morning, he would certainly die. We went back into theatre, but now the discontent in my mind grew alarmingly into a seed of bitterness. I felt I could stand no more.

Again, fortunately, I took my problem to the church elders for their prayers. Again they not only prayed for and comforted me, but also graciously rebuked me.

"Doctor, how many patients come to this hospital daily?"

I knew that only too well: I had to see them all.

"About two hundred to two hundred and fifty."

"All right. Why do they come?"

I didn't fall for that, and sat in gloomy silence.

"Surely they come because you are here! They wouldn't come if there were no doctor. And what are we doing?" – there was Agoya and his wife, Taadi, Bible School trained evangelists: Basuana and his wife Andugui, catechists from the Ibambi school: Nato, Mangadima's wife, and Naganimi, my friend, both trained Bible women – "all day, every day, wherever you go, we go. Wards, out-patients, health centre, leprosy care, maternity and child welfare clinics. Doctor, do you realise we are having the joy and privilege of leading five, ten, sometimes even more people to the Lord every week? If you weren't here they wouldn't come!"

Really what he was saying was that I bribed them to the hospital with medicine, and they wooed them into the Kingdom with love and preaching! God had to teach me to be willing to be a member of a team. I had wanted to write home in my prayer letters of how many I had led to the Lord (as I felt my prayer partners wanted to hear) and I had not thought that I could equally well tell them how many the team had brought into an assurance of salvation. As team members, we were each equally important to God, the individual role we played being no particular consequence.

The lesson was not learned overnight, simple though it seemed. Years later, the same problem arose in a different guise. After the suffering and destruction of the rebellion, when the way opened up for foreigners to return to help the nationals recommence the various aspects of their lives, the medical workers came together in consultation. The destruction of buildings and equipment was such as to daunt each member of the team contemplating the re-starting of the work on his own. The financial outlay would have been prohibitive. The frustrations when seeking to procure supplies and equipment would be almost insurmountable for each one alone. But if we came together and worked as a team, pooling our resources, our knowledge, our expertise, our enthusiasms and visions, could we not together achieve more than the sum of our individual efforts?

So the Nyankunde Evangelical Medical Centre was born!

My section of responsibility within the large complex was the training school for medical auxiliaries, nurses and midwives. I was back into the world of building, with plumbing and electrical installations added as a new bonus. As usual, I enjoyed it, and the challenge stretched my faith as we drew up somewhat ambitious plans. At the same time, all the course material for classes had to be up-graded and greatly increased. A team of us worked on this through the first four years, each evening preparing to-morrow's lectures in English, translating to French, checking, typing, duplicating, often working into the small hours, never able to get so much as a week ahead in the programme. Students had to be taught and supervised in theoretical and practical work. They had to be fed, clothed and housed. Recreational facilities had to be organised. Every day was full and varied.

Then others joined the team. There were those more qualified than I was to teach many of the first-year general subjects, as well as the art of nursing; others to teach pharmacy and laboratory techniques. Others organised sport and recreation, and supervised the feeding, clothing and housing of the students. There were several keen to assist in the morning Bible Study hour – and I slowly found that I was not really needed in the team in the way that I had been previously. This was hard to take. I had always been needed: I suppose my ego thrived on it. Now I was needed chiefly as a glorified office boy, cutting stencils and running the duplicator, writing government reports and letters, up-dating the school dossier regularly, calculating the annual statistics and maintaining some sort of filing system for all this material. I lived more and more in the office, less and less in either hospital or school room. My contacts with patients and with students were minimal. I understood ink better than medicines, typewriter better than stethoscope. And I was discontented.

As usual, the grumble reached the ears of the school committee, including two or three church elders. As usual they prayed for and encouraged me: and equally as usual they humbly rebuked me.

"Doctor," they said. "How many graduates have we from this school in full-time church service, out in the regional dispensaries?"

I knew that: my job was statistics!

"About thirty-seven at the present time," I answered.

"And they reach how many patients daily, do you suppose?"

According to our returns sheets, they were probably treating between three and four thousand patients daily, not counting the thousand at the Evangelical Medical Centre of Nyankunde.

"So three to four thousand patients are receiving good medical care daily, and are also hearing the Gospel regularly?"

I assented.

"Doctor, can't you see it?" they reasoned with me. "If you hadn't been here these last eighteen years or so, that would not be true! The government demands that a qualified doctor, with a certain number of years of experience in tropical medicine, with a good knowledge of French as well as Swahili, be in charge of the school full-time. Every document that goes from here to the government offices has to have your signature. Each of these graduates who has received his training, and taken his exams, and obtained his diploma, had to have your signature. We *need* you!"

Yes, they needed my signature, I could see that: but I had hoped they needed more . . .?

Then they added: "You know, we can't all be the last link in the chain! How many are those thirty-seven leading to the Saviour each week?"

Tears filled my eyes. It was true. Maybe fifty, maybe as many as a hundred some weeks, found the Lord as Saviour, in one or other of the clinics, hospitals, maternity units, staffed by our graduates and church evangelists. When would I learn the secret of happy contented team work? Why did I always want to be the last link? If I would love the Lord with all my mind, I had to give Him all that I thought I knew or could do, and be willing for Him to place me anywhere within the team to do any job He chose for me. Only then would I experience true peace of mind.

So often He seemed to ask me to do jobs for which I felt I was not trained – as builder, motor mechanic, plumber, secretary – that I hardly realised what He was doing when on one occasion He actually used my medical knowledge to work out His purposes.

On one of the long medical trips, visiting all our rural hospitals and dispensaries to the south of Nebobongo, I was on the last leg of the journey homewards. I had stopped at a M'Bari village, north of the Ituri river for a final clinic. It was a hard area. Missionaries had been working for many years in the region, but there had been little response. The tribe was warlike, the ancient centre of the vicious leopard cult, involving murder and cannibalism. There was one African evangelist and his wife, Anna, but they were discouraged by the hardness of the peoples' hearts and their refusal to accept the Word into their lives.

At that clinic, two patients of interest were brought to see me. One was Anna herself, expecting her fifth child. Her other four babies had all been born there in that forest village and each had died at birth. Her husband asked that she return with me to Nebobongo where by God's Grace I might help her to have a living baby. I gladly agreed to do what I could.

The second was a teenage girl with an enormous swelling in her neck. I examined her carefully, and in the absence of toxic symptoms or signs of pressure, decided firmly against the advisability of surgery. Under our still-primitive hospital conditions, and with my own very limited surgical knowledge and skill, the risk of an operation was far higher than the risk of keeping the goitre. But the mother was determined and pleaded with me for help. The best I could offer her was transport with us to a government hospital fifty miles to the north of Nebobongo. Ultimately we agreed to this.

We drove home, the remaining eighty miles, northwards across the wild gold-mine mountains of Babeyru, from M'Bari land to M'Budu land. For the M'Bari girl and her mother, it was their first journey ever out of their own tribal territory, and thus a journey fraught with fear, due to legendary tales of atrocities enacted in years past by the savage northern tribesmen against their southern neighbours. After a couple of weeks, I drove the two of them to the government hospital in Isiro.

Three weeks later, one Sunday afternoon, a car drove up to my front door. By the time I arrived from Sunday School in the nearby church, the car had left, but lying on a rush mat on the gravel drive, I saw the dead body of the teenage girl. My heart lurched. Bandages on her neck and at both elbows indicated that she had died during surgery, presumably from uncontrollable haemorrhage and a failure to maintain adequate blood transfusions. I could picture the scene: the very thing I had feared would happen had I tried to operate myself. But why? Why?

My mind was racing ahead. I had hopefully planned that by this M'Bari girl's physical recovery in a northern M'Budu or Miogo hospital, the way would be opened to the hearts of those southern tribesmen. They would be constrained to listen and respond to the Gospel brought to them by northern M'Budu evangelists. Now the door was slammed harder shut than ever. Why had God failed to seize this magnificent opportunity?

As I was thinking thus, the drums were beating, sending the news of the death of the girl rapidly southwards, across the mountain range. The mother was kneeling by her daughter's body, racked with bitter sobs, and the talking drums stirred her to fresh wailing, as fear welled up in her eyes. How would she be received home? She had allowed her M'Bari daughter to be "knifed to death" by a M'Budu devil!

Our evangelist came and stood beside me. He took it all in at a glance, and quietly asked me when I would set out in the car to take the body home to that southern village.

"Oh, no!" I ejaculated. "She must be buried here. To risk that treacherous journey for the living is one thing, but not for the dead." I was thinking of the rock-strewn mountain track, the rotten planks over hazardous rivers, the herds of wild elephants, the angry warlike tribesmen with their deadly accurate marksmanship – all spelt danger to car and driver alike.

"Doctor, please," Agoya pleaded. He had actually served as a missionary in M'Bari land for two years. He knew what he was saying to me. "You MUST go. You do not understand. To bury her here could mean tribal warfare."

How easily that can be repeated out of its setting: but heard there in the atmosphere of tribal bitterness and jealousies, a cold fear went through me. Slowly he persuaded me, and the journey was made. God protected us throughout. But bitter anger and resentment filled the one hundred and eighty people in that tribal village area.

The same week, ironically enough, a midwife came to report to me after the Tuesday morning ante-natal clinic, that Anna's baby was lying in such a way as to make a normal birth virtually impossible. With a heavy heart, I went to see her and attempted in vain to turn the yet-unborn baby. Eventually I gave in, and wrote Anna up for an operation the following Thursday, an elective lower-segment Caesarian section. Nothing very serious in that, back in the well-equipped hospitals of Britain, by a capable experienced surgeon, with excellent sterilising facilities and the availability of needed antibiotics or drugs to meet any possible complication during or after the operation: but it was a very different matter at Nebobongo.

I felt so very inexperienced: the hospital suddenly seemed very primitive and ill-equipped, despite all our efforts. The danger to the mother and the baby was alarmingly high. Again the dreaded questions surged into my thoughts. "Why, Lord? Why? Why Anna? Couldn't it have been someone else? Could you not have given Anna a living baby some other way, and vindicated Your Name to that M'Bari village?" There seemed to be a complete silence, a perceptible hush.

I operated. It was one of those strangely moving occasions when I was deeply conscious that Someone else operated, using my hands. I seemed to stand back and watch. It was relatively simple and straightforward. A lovely seven-pound baby boy was delivered, duly named Nehemiah, in thanksgiving to God for His gracious gift.

Nine weeks later, Anna and her husband left with their baby, to set out on a six-day journey home, walking over the mountain trails, to the same village to which some ten weeks previously, I had returned the dead body of the teenage girl.

They arrived at midday, fearful of their reception. They stood nervously in the little palaver hut by the big talking drum. Slowly the men of the village gathered round them in the open courtyard. The headman stepped forward and spoke.

"You have a baby?"

"Yes."

"Show us your baby."

The father took the baby from Anna's arms and passed it to the headman who examined the child in silence. The babe was then passed silently round the circle and back to the father.

"You had an operation?" – the talking drums had already told them.

"Yes."

"Show us the scar" – a typical African request.

Anna undid her skirt briefly and showed the scar.

Then God stepped in. Within the week, the village had turned to the Lord and accepted Christ as Saviour. Whatever had happened? What had brought about this change of heart? How had God intervened? I certainly had not operated in order to bring a village to the Lord, but somewhat resentfully, feeling that God had not properly understood the situation.

It would seem that God had merely asked me to give Him my mind, my training, the ability that He had given me, to serve Him unquestioningly and to leave with Him the consequences. And He was thinking, not merely as an African, but actually as a M'Bari African. He understood their thought patterns as I never would. They had seen the pagan girl go to a government hospital, have an operation and die. Now a Christian woman went to a Christian hospital, had to have an operation to "complete the parallelism", and LIVED. And they accepted Him, her God, as their God, seeing Him as the all-powerful God.

How wonderful God is, and how foolish we are to argue with Him and not to trust Him wholly in every situation as we seek to serve Him!

Turning from this dramatic story to the more usual and humdrum situations of everyday life, teaching medical skills and seeking to pass on my knowledge to Africans with very little educational background, became my main outlet in seeking to serve God with all my mind. Having completed one year of general secondary education, John Mangadima had come to me as a teenager, bright eyed and keen. "Teach me to be a doctor" had been his plea, which became my most exciting challenge. Could I pass on to African students the mind-training that I had been privileged to receive? Could God instil into African youths the sense of high vocation and responsibility that medical service would demand? Could God use me in this ministry? Was I willing to trust God to do it by giving Him "all my mind" to use as He wished?

John and I worked together for many years in the effort to fulfil that vision. He helped me learn Swahili, so keen was he to understand me when I taught him medicine! He was indefatigable. He came out every night to see every emergency case, whether he was on duty or not. He would ask to borrow my stethoscope in the evening and go back to the ward to listen-in again to a chest rumble or a heart murmur to which I had drawn attention on the morning round, to fix it in his mind. He asked endless questions, such as: "What makes the mercury go up the tube when a patient has fever?" and again: "Why did you give that patient sulphonamide and this one penicillin, and yet you say they both have a chest infection?"

He did so well in his first qualifying exams as an orderly, that the examiners, a couple of government doctors, raised their eyebrows when he left the room after his official oral test. Someone expressed surprise that a "native" had such a grip of the reason for his actions, not just a rote method of blind unreasoning obedience to a formula.

John married an intelligent girl in the local school, and the two went to Bible School. They did well. They put all they'd got into becoming good servants of the Lord Jesus Christ. In their last term, each was senior student of the men and women's groups. They graduated with a real knowledge of, and love for, the Word of God: and were appointed to Nebobongo to work with me in the hospital as medical evangelists.

We had not had a national co-worker before on the medical team, and we had many lessons to learn. The custom of many years was that the foreign medical personnel held the key to the pharmacy and dispensed all the drugs. Now we had a national colleague. Obviously John's training was much less than ours, his knowledge still very limited: but as a colleague, should he not also be trusted with access to all medicines? Small though our monthly allowances were, they were still vastly greater than what John earned: could we find a way to narrow the difference? Because I was a white foreigner, I commanded immediate respect, in those colonial days, both from white administrators and black patients. Patients still wanted to see the "white doctor". How could we help to build up their respect for one of their own tribe? Yes, we had problems, but God graciously gave us the will and determination to conquer those same problems and go on beyond them.

John was a national, and I was keen to encourage him to be proud of being an African. He wanted to help his own people, and I did all I could to make this possible. At times, it almost led to confrontation, for example over the salaries paid to our nurses and workmen. My method was to see what money was available, and then divide it between every one, maintaining minimal differentials. But there was a government scale of minimum wages. I never seriously considered this. Our team had all signed private contracts with us, and they were not government employees. We simply did not have the sort of money necessary to pay a government work force. I was not unduly concerned, as I knew that all the side benefits that our people received – free medical care, housing, feeding, clothing, free schooling for their children, a congenial atmosphere, time allowed for all church activities – more than made up the difference.

Black thinking was not as mine! "Basic salary", hard cash, was measurable. In their minds, fringe benefits were my gifts to them, and therefore did not affect the situation. How could I call it a gift if I then deducted it from salary? And had they not the right to choose to starve if they wished, and use the cash to buy a coveted bicycle? What right had I to compel them to eat, by issuing a food ration? I was very very ignorant in the ways of arbitration, and very lacking in patient diplomacy when dealing with the "floor workers". John became an able trade-union leader, in his own amateur way! My conscience hindered me in bargaining – *was* I being wholly fair? *Was* I altogether right? *Would* the government approve, as I assured them was the case? The Bible taught me all my dealings and all my speech were

to be without guile – without the slightest smear of hypoc-
risy or pretence of falsehood.

We made our way through, and kept on going on. Independence brought a crop of new problems. Who was
actually, ultimately, in charge? White or black? "Foreign
neo-colonial western imperialists" as the radio daily called all
whites, or a new well-qualified, capable national, only "held
down by the white dictator and made to feel less qualified
and incapable, because the white feared to lose his power",
as the radio daily declared? My mind reeled under the effect
of the continuous brain-washing and insidious innuendoes,
and I wondered just how long I would be able to stay?
John's own spiritual growth and humility solved that set of
problems. He knew his abilities, that he was a medical assistant and not a qualified doctor, and he did not want more
responsibility than he could carry. He was willing to take
over a little more of the administrative work. He was keen to
learn anything more of the medical and surgical work that I
would teach him: but he did not seek a title beyond his
capabilities.

I began to teach him to teach, so that he should take over
the lectures to the first-year students, in anatomy and physiology, first aid, and basic medical concepts and vocabulary,
and the rudiments of the practical art of nursing. He learned
well and quickly. His mind was keen, and he appreciated
that it was one thing to know something, but another thing
to know how to pass that knowledge on to others. He had lost
all sense of inferiority towards me, of difference because of
the colour of our skins, or the extent of our training. We
were a team, pulling together, yoked together by Christ's
spirit, with a common goal and purpose. He accepted me as
myself, and wasted little time troubling about our differ-
ences. It was the same in the church as in the classroom.

He learned avidly all I loved to teach and share of my knowledge of the Scriptures, in order that he might pass it on.

But this happy relationship was not always appreciated by others. One day, in a physiology class, when we were studying the structure and work of the eye, we were both saddened to realise that our African companions were still easily hurt by white "superiority" of knowledge, if not of behaviour. It was such a small incident, and we fell into the mistake so innocently and thoughtlessly. I had a model of the eye. I had covered the blackboard with diagrams. I had shown them the inside of a camera, the shutter, the lens, the dark space, the moving film. We had talked of the developing process and the production of a photograph of what had been "seen". Then John, remembering past years, asked me to show them the "diagram in your book". I turned and took down volume two of an anatomy/physiology English text-book, and opened at a page in the "one thousand two hundred" section. It was a good, clearly labelled diagram, even though in English, which language they did not understand.

I felt the atmosphere. There was a sudden change, from the warm sunny sense of friendship, alertness and keenness to learn. Sadness had come in. A heavy look of depression, of frustration, settled over their faces, A barrier was put up between us. They had a 52-page duplicated anatomy/physiology text-book, alternate pages in 4-colour diagrams which they filled in and labelled. They had felt they were getting somewhere. Their knowledge and understanding was increasing, when the white doctor nonchalantly turned up page 1,200 and something, and showed them a fantastic and beautiful diagram with HUNDREDS of labels. They felt they knew nothing. They never would know anything. What was the point of trying? She was only condescending to their stupidity and offering them a sop to their pride. It was all so futile.

John felt it. I was grieved for them, sorry I had inadvertently hurt them, wishing I'd had the sense to think first. John was annoyed. When would the students cease to be so childish, and accept themselves for what they were, and me for what I was? When would they give up making odious comparisons, and be wholly content to do all they could to bring the two images more nearly into focus?

We learned surgery together, through sheer necessity. I had the text-book and the basic theoretical knowledge: John had the hands and an inborn surgical skill and sensitivity. He learned quickly and well. The repair of hernias of every shape and size became our weekly diet. I planned to do as few as were essential to the saving of life, on the one hand, and the training of a surgical team, ready for emergencies, on the other. John pressed me to do the maximum number possible, in order to develop skill and confidence. God graciously blessed our efforts, and together with the nursing team, we were enabled to help some two hundred and fifty critically ill patients during a four-year period.

Many others took part in the training programme, without whom John would never have succeeded. He came for two years to Nyankunde after the rebellion, and worked hard at the new advanced teaching, in French rather than Swahili, and did well. He learned general medicine and diagnostic procedures under Dr. Carl Becker and Dr. Harry Wilke: he learned basic surgical techniques and many essential procedures under Dr. Herb Atkinson and Dr. Dick Ulrich: he learned the art of normal midwifery and the skill of rightly timed surgical intervention in maternity care from Dr. Ruth Dix.

Now to-day, he is the director of our Nebobongo hospital, and the general supervisor of the work at Malingwia and

Mulito hospitals to the far north and south of the area, some one thousand miles apart. Along with a team of six missionary nurse/midwives and eighteen or twenty national paramedical auxiliary workers, John carries the responsibility of all the rural clinics and dispensaries supported by these three hospitals. He does major surgical interventions under the authority of the qualified medical staff at the Evangelical Medical Centre, three hundred and fifty miles away. Together, white foreigner and black national see to the organisation and supervision of African nursing and paramedical staff, the ordering and provision of medicines and equipment, the representation of the medical service to the government authorities, and the preparation of annual statistical reports.

However exciting this mental exercise of training national workers, and preparing them for the role of medical leadership, it was not only in this somewhat dramatic way that God taught me to serve Him with all my mind and such mental ability as He had given me. He asked also for humble acceptance of, and willingness for, the more routine jobs of office work, statistics, reports, letters, forms: the use of a God-given ability to work with figures. For my last three years in Africa I did little else, and I confess I frequently grumbled, feeling my "gifts" were not being used, and that it was an uneconomical use of personnel to put a qualified doctor/surgeon, college lecturer and director into an office. Once again, God was teaching me that obedience is all He asks for, and an honest willingness to be a team member, however humble the role.

Nyelongo, one of the masons trained by Basuana, as we built the Nyankunde medical auxiliary training school, gave a lovely testimony of how he and his wife came to know the Lord as their Saviour. He was late to work one morning, and missed roll-call. When I came out of school at 8.15 a.m.

after the second teaching period, I went to see that all was well at the building site, as was my custom. Nyelongo was afraid that I would be annoyed with him. On the contrary, quite spontaneously, I went straight to him, and asked about his baby. He was startled, not realising that I knew that they had a new baby.

"The baby is very sick," he replied.

He continued his testimony: "You asked me where the baby was, and then you were really annoyed when I told you that the baby was at home because we couldn't afford the hospital admission card. You went straight up to your house, came charging down again in the Land-Rover, directly on to the building site, and told me to get in."

He reminded me how I had driven at once to his village, and brought the mother and baby back to hospital, and given him time off until the baby began to recover. At the end of the month, when he came with the other workmen for his pay packet, he was nervously plucking up courage to ask me to spread his debt over several months, rather than taking that whole month's salary, when I called his name and handed him his usual pay packet.

Astonished he ran home to his wife in the next valley. Together they had counted it. It was all there, no deduction at all.

"We cried," he said. "We knelt down, as we suddenly realised all that you and Basuana meant when you told us day after day of God's love: and we asked God then and there into our hearts and lives, and have followed Him ever since."

Very probably when I made up the wage packets that month, I had simply forgotten that Nyelongo owed money. That is not the point. As God was able to use my service (willing or unwilling) in doing the office work involved in paying the workmen, using my mind to fill in their record sheets and count out the cash and balance the accounts, so He had planned to reach Nyelongo's heart in the way He saw best: and I became a tool in His hand, an arrow to find its mark in a workman's heart and life.

## Chapter 4

# With ALL my strength

*"My Grace is sufficient for you, for my power is made perfect in weakness." I will all the more gladly boast of my weaknesses, that the power of Christ may rest upon me.*
II. COR. 12: 9

SLOWLY GOD TAUGHT the lessons inherent in living and working as a team, giving Him heart and soul and mind and body, that He might reach others with His love. Making bricks was probably one of the earliest lessons here. I remember when we burned our first kiln. We had under-estimated the amount of firewood that we would need. The kiln was half-fired, when I saw there was not enough to complete the job. All that had already been burned would be wasted, if the fire went out and had to be re-kindled. The only possible way to avoid this wastage was for EVERYONE in the village to down tools, and gather firewood for twenty-four hours to enable us to complete the firing.

I moved fast. I asked the senior teacher in the primary school to organise the one hundred children into a chain to carry wood. I sought the help of every able-bodied relative of patients in the hospital and waiting women in the maternity unit to help us for the day, promising a day's free treatment for the patient in lieu of the normal payment. I selected a skeleton team to staff the wards, sending most of the student nurses and pupil midwives off into the adjacent forest area with axes. All the workmen and their wives were called in from other jobs, and joined the "emergency task force".

Then I took an axe and went down with them to the forest, and cut vigorously for an hour. I was strong and well able to swing an axe, and eventually cut up the tree trunk on which I was working into six sizeable chunks. My hands were badly blistered though, from the unaccustomed exercise. A midwife showed me how to plait a vine and hoist a chunk on to my back, slung round my head with the twisted band: and I led off a procession of now-singing young folk, amused and encouraged by my being with them. On the second journey, they insisted on photographing "their doctor" carrying firewood, saying they were sure my Mother had never seen me doing that back home – and how right they were! Yet it was a small part of "loving Him with my body", that is with all the strength that He had given me.

Early in my missionary life, I had been challenged by the verse: "May the God of peace Himself sanctify you wholly; and may your spirit and soul and body be kept sound and blameless at the coming of our Lord Jesus Christ" (I Thess. 5: 23).

I felt keenly that we should train ourselves and our national co-workers to love Him and glorify Him in and with our bodies, as much as with our minds trained in the classroom, and with our spirits trained in the church Bible Study groups. In presenting the Gospel of our Lord Jesus Christ, I wanted them to understand that God wanted their bodies as much as their spirits: that they are ONE in God's eyes, and that He desired total surrender and total allegiance. The Bible teaches that "those who worship Him must worship in spirit" (John 4: 24) but it also teaches: "Glorify God in your body" (I Cor. 6: 20). It stresses also that I am to love God with all my body as much as with all my mind and spirit. My body is "God's temple, and ... God's Spirit dwells in me" (I Cor. 3: 16). So I wanted to help them to understand that God asked for healthy strong pure bodies as much as well-developed disciplined minds, and Biblically taught, worshipful spirits.

So we had a football team at Nebobongo. I taught them and coached them on Wednesday afternoons, with the aid of an F.A. rule book and a knowledge of hockey! On Saturdays we played matches against anyone willing to play with us. We soon found that there were plenty of lessons here, as to how to be a Christian on the football field: how to develop a spirit of fair play rather than hoping to get away with a foul without the referee seeing: and especially how to lose to an away team with a good grace!

Teaching purity and chastity as God-given precepts was no easier and no more acceptable in another culture than in one's own. In fact, there were many added difficulties, especially where local custom accepted trial marriages, and where a girl, who had already had a baby, was more eligible for marriage than one who had not. It was on a level of sacrificial obedience to God's commandments that this standard for a holy church "in splendour, without spot or wrinkle or any such thing, that she might be holy and without blemish" (Eph. 5: 27), had to be understood.

Our different cultural backgrounds gave us differing gifts to share with each other. The Africans were stoical in the face of pain. I had met this in my first year in the country, in many varying forms in the dispensary and hospital. At first, we had had no means of anaesthesia. To see an elderly man take a grip of himself whilst I pulled out the roots of three broken teeth: to watch an eleven-year-old pigmy boy grit his teeth and suck in his breath, whilst I had to re-break a badly united fracture of his thigh bone: to observe the deep pain in the eyes of a mother hour after hour during a very difficult complicated confinement: each one had challenged me with their quiet powers of endurance.

I was afraid of pain. During the rebellion, that fear came

harshly to the fore. I was not afraid of dying, but I was afraid of the pain that might be inflicted before I died. Once when a man raised a spear to drive it through me, I just prayed that I might die with the first blow: I could not bear the thought of mutilation and lingering agony in death. The night of the 29th October when the rebel lieutenant pressed a gun to my forehead and cursed me and threatened to kill me, I prayed that he would pull the trigger. It would have been quick and easy, easier than going on living.

That was the moment Hugh, a seventeen-year-old, first year student, had broken loose from two soldiers holding him out on the road. He had thrown himself between me and the lieutenant, shouting: "You don't touch her, except over my dead body." They had beaten him up savagely, and thrown him out as dead, and kicked his inert body around as a football. I had been sick, sensing that a teenager had given his life for me. That he lived was a miracle: but that he voluntarily suffered such awful pain out of his love and loyalty to me, was to me an even greater miracle.

I was no longer praying. I was beyond praying. I held on to the Name of Jesus. Someone back home must have been praying earnestly for me. If I had prayed any prayer, it would have been: "My God, my God, why hast Thou forsaken me?"

Then, quietly, God met with me. He had reminded me that twenty years before I had asked for the privilege of being a missionary. "This is it. Don't you want it?" He seemed to say to me.

The fantastic privilege of being identified with our Saviour dawned afresh in my heart.

He had asked me for the loan of my body. He had not taken away the pain or the cruelty or the humiliation. No, it had still been there, all there, yet it suddenly became quite different. In the depth of my weakness, He revealed His strength. It was now – with Him, in Him, for Him. It had been triumphant victory in the midst of apparent defeat. Joy had come for tears. Privilege had displaced all sense of cost.

Then rebel soldiers had tried to take John Mangadima's seven-year-old daughter Ebenezeri and my adopted ten-year-old daughter Fibi, to make them "slaves of the regime". My fear fell away, and I fought fiercely to keep the two girls out of their clutches. I would have done anything, like a furious mother hen defending her chickens! And I learned a little more of loving with all my strength, and how strength comes in response of the demands of love.

Together we learned why God has given us His Name as "I AM". His Grace always proved itself sufficient in the moment of need, but never before time, and rarely afterwards. As I anticipated suffering in my imagination and thought of what these cruel soldiers would do next, I quivered with fear. I broke out in a cold sweat of horror. As I heard them drive into our village, day or night, my mouth would go dry: my heart would miss a beat. Fear gripped me in an awful vice. But when the moment came for action, He gave me a quiet cool exterior that He used to give others courage too: He filled me with a peace and an assurance as to what to say or do, that amazed me and often defeated the immediate tactics of the enemy.

When the rebels would leave the village, reaction often set in. I would feel limp and nerveless. Many times, I felt I just couldn't bear any more. The stress was unbelievable. As I looked back over the previous half hour or whatever, it all seemed unreal. Often we could hardly believe that we were still alive. We knew it was not our wisdom or strength that had brought us through. Even while I was marvelling at what the Lord had just achieved for us, already I was fearing the testing that would come next.

Following our rescue from the rebellion, and after a year

at home to recover equilibrium, we went back to join our African colleagues in the mammoth task of reconstruction. Medically I had been warned. The rebellion, coming after four years of physical, mental and spiritual strain during which we had known long periods of hunger, and equally long periods of a tremendously heavy work load, had taken a toll. I was told that I needed to slow down, to slacken the pace. I was strongly advised to seek to share the load, and to make no effort to get under the whole burden again alone.

"If you will not heed our warning, we cannot be responsible for the outcome," said the doctors.

The needs clamoured on all sides. Anything that had been done in previous years seemed minuscule in comparison to what needed to be done in 1966. There were thousands of patients, and hardly any drugs. Hospital buildings were derelict. Our para-medical workers had all returned to their own villages, and there was no money available to pay their salaries. Yet the patients were there.

There were thousands of refugees, and hardly any food. Camps had to be erected and organised. Government and Christian organisations sent clothing, bedding, food, but its distribution needed supervision, and careful planning so that the right people received it. Many church leaders were not yet released from rebel captivity: others had been killed. There were so few to carry responsibility and to do the jobs. Yet the refugees were there.

There were thousands of children, and hardly any schools. All buildings and equipment had been maliciously destroyed. There were no blackboards nor chalk, no exercise books nor pencils. There were few school masters willing to start teaching again with no promise of a salary. Two years of schooling had been lost, and during that time, children had inevitably lost the ground gained in the previous one or two years. We had therefore three or four years to make up, and if there were to be any recovery, this was an urgent need. But who would tackle it?

God gave strength in our weakness. That year, the more we looked around us, the more we saw need. The more we saw need, the more conscious we were of our own inability and weakness. Yet looking back on that year, we marvel as we realise how He enabled, pouring in His strength and bringing about His purposes.

The hospital was repaired. The para-medical workers re-assembled. Lectures recommenced. Somehow drug supplies were obtained. Thousands of patients were treated. Morale rose, and a new courage flowed.

Refugee centres were set up by different missionaries here and there. Local workers were selected and trained. Literally hundreds of tons of food and clothing were systematically and conscientiously distributed to the thousands of needy refugees, enabling them to come to grips with the situation, and start living again.

Schools re-opened. Masters were encouraged to accept what little money was available, knowing that we were doing everything possible to move the Government to speed up essential subsidies. Equipment was bought in the capital and shipped up-country, and prayed to its destination. Thousands of children were organised into hundreds of classes, and amazingly, discipline was speedily restored, and order began to emerge out of chaos.

We gathered to thank God for pouring His strength into and through our weakness. We gave Him all the limited strength of our own physical, mental and spiritual resources, as an act of love, and He graciously accepted the love-gift, and poured out His blessing upon the offering.

There were other lessons to be learned in this context. Giving Him my strength was not really hard. It was a joy to have any to give. I liked hard work. I was happy to be able to show God that I loved Him by my willing service. Then He asked me to allow Him to exchange my strength for weakness. I did not recognise His voice, and could not understand what He was saying, or doing.

First, it was a question of physical strength: later it involved also the ideas of strength of character.

I became physically ill. During my years in Africa, I frequently became ill, often quite seriously so. During the first five years, besides recurrent bouts of tonsillitis and malaria, I had fairly severe amoebic dysentery complicated by hepatitis. Jessie Scholes, Amy Grant and many others spent a lot of time nursing me and looking after my physical needs. Then in 1957, during the only two months that I was alone (so far as white missionaries were concerned) at Nebobongo, I was very ill indeed, with either meningitis or cerebral malaria. John Mangadima, my newly appointed medical assistant, made the diagnosis and started treatment. The evangelist Agoya organised a twenty-four hour, round-the-clock prayer vigil in the church. My cook and house-lad did all they could to help me. A team of student nurses saw to my medical needs.

I recovered and thanked them all for their loving care. They could not have done more for me if I'd been one of their own tribe.

In my second term, I had a second bout of cerebral malaria and was ill for three months. During the first ten days of raging fever and delirium, Suzanne, one of the first qualified girl nurses, never left me. She "specialled" me day and night. Nothing was too much trouble for her. Cold sponges and bed baths, drip feeding and intravenous therapy, prayer and immeasurable tender loving care all ministered to my ultimate recovery. Others laundered and dried bed-linen day after day as I sweated out the course of the fever. The team cared, and was concerned, and quietly took the burden of my recovery on their hearts. My missionary colleagues, Florence and Elaine, carried the responsibilities of all the hospital work, refusing to burden me with that during those long weeks. Eventually I was moved to Ibambi, where Muriel Harman gave me devoted nursing care for a further month. Then I went to convalesce at Egbita where missionary friends, Agnes and Marjorie, gave unstinted hours to encourage my eventual recovery.

In my third term, I had tick-borne typhus fever and nervous exhaustion. Now at our Nyankunde Medical Centre, I had the loving service of a competent team of workers. Abisayi personally checked the blood slides and did the cell counts. Lobo himself saw that the right drugs were sent up according to prescription. Dr. Becker visited me daily: Vera came twice daily to give injections. Students from the training college slept in my sitting room so that I should not be alone at nights (until I was moved first to Dr. Ruth Dix's home, and later down to the hospital.) Juneno, a third-year girl student, "specialled" me, and sat up most of the first two nights watching the drip, calming my restlessness and helping me during the violent bouts of vomiting. Irene had me in her home for a month, later on, for convalescence. Everyone did so much for me.

Again I recovered and again I thanked all for their loving care. But there were unanswered questions in my heart.

Each time I was ill, another, African or missionary, who already had a full work-load, had to give time to care for me. Someone else had to undertake my work in addition to their own. After each illness I became so depressed and discouraged, sensing that I was becoming a burden to the team and should go home. What was God trying to say to me?

Each time I was ill, Africans and missionaries nursed me and cared for me, poured out their love and prayed me back to health and strength. The Africans were largely those whom I myself had helped to train, graduates and students of our para-medical auxiliary schools.

Why could God not keep me in good health? Of course, He could, but why did He not choose to do this?

I was very slow to appreciate the answer to this question. He was inviting me to share in a type of sacrifice for which I could see no relevance then. Through these repeated episodes of illness, my general health was slowly undermined. I had very little resistance left, and no reserve energy to call upon in times of emergency need. The wearying anaemia associated with the various diseases was not responding to simple treatment. The nervous tension of living in a developing country in the early years of its independence, with all the uncertainties and political anxieties was telling on me, so that I could not relax or sleep. Why? I was sure there was a spiritual explanation but I found it hard to understand, and hard to roll the burden on to the Lord, as many exhorted me to do.

Since I first went to Africa, I had prided myself that all my needs were met by and in the Lord Jesus Christ. I felt it was wrong to "need" Africans (or missionaries) and deliberately to set out to win the affection of students or others to satisfy that need. I considered that my natural need of the security of being loved should be wholly satisfied by God's love, and the certainty that He loved me. Then I was free to love the students and others, not primarily for the return I would receive, but to show them His love and draw them to Him.

Basically I believe that was a true aspiration, but there was a flaw. Each one of us likes to be wanted, needed, even needs to be needed. No-one would choose to do a job where he knew he was not needed. It would be demoralising. For years I was the only missionary doctor in our area, and so I was always needed. I was thus on the giving end, and the

African was on the receiving end, always saying "Thank you". This equally can soon become demoralising. I had not seen that the roles needed to be reversed if the Africans were to know the same sense of fulfilment and joy in being needed that I knew.

Only when I was ill, did I obviously, unequivocably, need them. There was no pretence then. They nursed me, they cared for me, they fed me, they washed me. And I said "Thank you" – and meant it.

To them it was a great joy that for once they knew without question that *they* were needed, and had a chance to show their love in willing service. They had a giving role and not just the usual receptive one.

But their joy in this instance lay not in my physical strength, but in my weakness. I believe this was part of the deeper meaning of "Love Me with all your strength" – that I must give my body, my strength, to God, even to sickness nigh unto death, that He might love others through me. I was to *give* Him the strength I had sought to develop, even accepting that He would replace it with weakness.

Secondly, God had to take me along the same sort of path with regard to strength of character as He had done with regard to physical strength. Would I give Him what appeared to be my strong points, my ability to lead, even my earnest desire to be utterly His, and let Him replace it all with a consciousness (a realisation) of weakness, so that He might be more wholly able to show forth His strength?

To love the Lord my God with all my strength might, paradoxically, mean to love Him wholly in my weakness. By giving to Him what I thought of as my strength, realising my actual weakness, He could then demonstrate His real strength.

"My Grace is sufficient for you, for My power is made perfect in weakness," took on new meaning.

It was often far from pleasant, this learning process. I

learned the frightening weakness of fear during the five months of rebel captivity, and it took an African brother, Basuana, to teach me to accept deliverance from fear, by faith in the unshakable Word of God. I learned that Christ could keep me calm and fill me with His peace, even while a storm of fear raged all around me.

I was shaken recently to learn again the frightening weakness of fear, and God had to show me again what "I" without Him am really like. It was a pretty despicable picture. I was going up to London to speak at an afternoon rally and evening meeting. I had driven by car to the nearest underground station, and was parking on a piece of waste land, amongst crowds of other vehicles. A huge lorry was impatiently waiting to get out. Another car swept by on my offside, which I had not even seen approaching. I panicked, accelerated too hard in reverse, and felt the dull thud of impact between my rear bumper and the passenger door of a parked yellow saloon car. I didn't stop to think, let alone pray. I drove away. Fear took over: fear of a bill I couldn't pay: fear of the loss of a no-claims-bonus: fear even of an endorsement for careless driving.

Eventually parked elsewhere, I caught the train to London, and then had time to reflect. I could hardly believe it. That *I* had done such a despicable thing – how often had I seen similar things done by others, and commented hotly on how mean they were – it was a rotten thing to do. Should I get out of the train, go back on the next, find the car, and leave my name and address under the windscreen wipers? I would be too late for the meeting. I was torn. The decision was made for me, as I found I was on an express train, Uxbridge to Baker Street.

After a miserable eight hours, I returned that evening to the car park and looked for the car. It had gone. There was no-one there, no official, no policeman. I returned next day, and for several following days. I found a policeman and reported the whole story. I did not know the make of car nor the registration number. I did all I could to put right the affair – to no avail. I merely found that I could do nothing to pay for the rottenness of my own corrupt nature. God reminded me quickly of the four wasted years of effort trying to earn forgiveness in the past, and I found I had to accept His strength, through forgiveness and cleansing, for all my weaknesses. I had to recognise and acknowledge that in me (as well as in others whom I see around me) lies no good thing, apart from His indwelling Presence. Only as I am daily willing for Him to crucify the self-life, the capital "I", can He live in and through me in His own triumphant, victorious life.

So often I seem to have to learn lessons over and over again. Yet God is so graciously willing to go on teaching, so patiently waiting to fill and overflow with His daily enabling by His indwelling Holy Spirit.

\*     \*     \*

As the branch to become the arrow has to lose its leaves and flowers, so I perhaps the pleasant home, a fixed salary and married joys: the ownership of books and pretty possessions, the indulgence in luxury foods or unnecessary accessories: the desire to feel needed or useful or to be employing one's so-called natural gifts to the full, rather than filling a niche in a team-programme. I needed to be willing to see Him dealing with all these as leaves and flowers. For each of us the specific areas which God will touch will be different, but the principle remains the same. There is nothing wrong with the leaves and flowers: on the contrary, they are essential to the life of the branch: but they are a hindrance, a weight, to a balanced arrow.

The side branches, thorns and knots must all be trimmed

away with the whittling knife to perfect the arrow. Likewise God is working on my temperament, my sensibilities, my habits – "the sin which clings so closely", as impatience, being hurt easily, unbelief, relying on my feelings, my pride of nationality, education and apparent natural abilities: my self – self-pity, or self-reliance, or self-justification: my cowardice to face myself for what I really am – to see myself as others see me.

Finally the bark has to be stripped, and the inner branch sand-papered to bring about the polished shaft, thus destroying the individuality of the branch, and attacking its own inherent strength to withstand all onslaughts of nature. The desire for my "rights" in order to preserve my individuality (rather than allowing God the full right to take over my life and to perfect my personality) has to be stripped away. I have to learn to persevere in the race He has set before me, drawing my strength only from Him, and not relying at all on what I may consider any natural abilities I may have. I have to let God take from me even that strength which I thought I had in order that He may more fully reveal His own strength: in order that He may continue in me the work of conforming me to the image of His Son.

Paul said: "I have been crucified with Christ: it is no longer I who live, but Christ who lives in me; and the life I now live in the flesh I live by faith in the Son of God, who loved me and gave Himself for me" (Gal. 2: 20).

This death-life, as seen in the imagery of the stripping of the branch to create the arrow, may appear to be full of sacrifices, and thus be a costly discipline. Yet as our Lord Himself told us there is no other way to the fullness of the abundant life that He would pour into us:

"I came that they may have life, and have it abundantly" and again:

"Truly, truly, I say to you, unless a grain of wheat falls

into the earth and dies, it remains alone; but if it dies, it bears much fruit" (John 10: 10 and 12: 24).

I long to be kept by God in an attitude of willing surrender so that He can go on to perfect that which concerns me; that He can go on stripping and whittling and sandpapering until He is content with the new arrow He is creating.

Crucifixion, the death-to-self life, must surely be seen by us all as costly, but the abundant life that He wishes to bestow on each can only be seen as unutterable privilege.

"This slight momentary affliction is preparing for us an eternal weight of glory beyond all comparison" (II Cor. 4: 17).

# My privilege to respond

*Through Him then let us continuously offer up a sacrifice of praise to God ... Do not neglect to do good and to share what you have, for such sacrifices are pleasing to God.*

HEB. 13: 15, 16

*While the people pressed upon Him to hear the Word of God, He was standing by the Lake of Gennesaret. And He saw two boats by the lake; but the fishermen had gone out of them and were washing their nets. Getting into one of the boats, which was Simon's, He asked him to put out a little from the land. And He sat down and taught the people from the boat.*

*And when He had ceased speaking, He said to Simon, "Put out into the deep and let down your nets for a catch."*

*And Simon answered, "Master, we toiled all night and took nothing! But at your word, I will let down the nets."* Luke 5: 1–5.

They were asked to push out in faith into the deep, no toe on the bottom. And it was mid-morning. As fishermen, they knew there could be no fish swimming in the upper waters at that time. To let down their nets now would make them the laughing stock of the crowd on the shore: it was against all common sense. They were tired, too, after a fruitless night of labour. Yet ... He had asked it of them. They did as He bid, and enclosed a great multitude of fishes. Fear and respect, astonishment and excitement fought for supremacy in their thoughts.

*"Do not be afraid: henceforth you will be catching men."*
*And when they had brought their boats to land, they left*
*everything and followed Him.* Luke 5: 10, 11.

There was no other possible response: "they left
EVERYTHING and followed Him." They forsook ALL.
Would that renunciation be considered as *sacrifice* by
others?

\*     \*     \*

In conclusion, let us remind ourselves of that one "full, perfect and sufficient Sacrifice" of our Saviour, as He gave
Himself in obedience to the will of His Father "unto death,
even the death of the Cross".

He bore my sins on His body on the tree.

He died that I might be forgiven, healed by His stripes.

There was no other sinless One who could have redeemed
us: there is no other Name under heaven by which men must
be saved.

He died once for all – for all sins, for all men, for all time.
He cried: "It is finished." There can be no further sacrifice
for sin.

Then what is my part? How can I respond? What
sacrifice can I make to Him and for Him, to show the depth
of my love in response to all He has done for me?

The Psalmist declares that he will offer to God *a sacrifice
of thanksgiving* as he calls on His Name. The writer to the
Hebrews exhorts them to offer up continually *sacrifices of
praise* to God as they acknowledge His Name. He stresses
that doing good and sharing what we have with others, less
well provided for, are *"sacrifices pleasing to God"* (Heb.
13: 15, 16). Likewise, Paul calls the financial aid that he received from the Philippians *"a sacrifice acceptable and
pleasing to God"* (Phil. 4: 18).

The Christians in Asia Minor at that time were facing persecution and torture for their faith. They were exhorted nevertheless to have courage to acknowledge publicly that they were followers of Christ. Meeting together before dawn or after dark, for worship and prayer, could well result in martyrdom at the stake or in the arena. The despised sect of Christians was branded as illegal by imperial Rome, who attempted to force members to recant, and to sacrifice an animal on a pagan shrine to the Emperor of the day, as to a god. The Christians would rather die! They continued to offer to God their sacrifices of praise and thanksgiving, even if it led them to their death.

To do good to others in that decadent age when all thought only of their own comfort and advancement was an attitude of heart and mind so foreign to the culture of the day, that Roman soldiers, sent to search out the secret groups of Christian believers, came back to the authorities baffled. They could find nothing with which to accuse these Christians. All they did was good. The only vows they took were those in which they promised not to defraud others and to pay their debts promptly. Out of their poverty, they shared with others who had even less. To God their way of life was a pleasing sacrifice.

In a different age and different cultures, William Carey, Hudson Taylor, C. T. Studd, Mary Slessor, William Booth and a host of others made "sacrifices well-pleasing to God". With hearts aflame with love for God, they launched out around the world, to preach the Gospel to those who had never heard it. "If Jesus Christ be God, and died for me, then no sacrifice can be too great for me to make for Him." Thus could be summed up the driving power behind the outpoured service of each one.

The night I was converted, I was given a word of direction for my Christian life from Phil. 3: 10: "That I may know

Christ, and the power of His Resurrection and may share His sufferings, becoming like Him in His death." In its setting that verse is all the more demanding and remarkable. Paul, a doctor of law and philosophy, a respected member of the Sanhedrin, a revered leader of the people, "had it made", as we would say to-day. He would never need to think about how to pay the mortgage or educate his children, or provide for the family in his old age. He need never fear redundancy or unemployment. Then he met with the Lord Jesus Christ. His life was revolutionised. He suddenly had a new goal, a new purpose, a new zeal and fervour. "Whatever gain I had," he said, "I count it as loss for the sake of Christ. Indeed I count everything as loss because of the surpassing worth of knowing Christ Jesus my Lord. For His sake I have suffered the loss of all things, and count them as refuse, in order that I may gain Christ" (Phil. 3: 7, 8). Paul gave up ALL in order to follow Christ, and to take the Good News to Asia Minor and Greece and Italy. "Sacrifices well-pleasing to God."

The early Christians in the first and second centuries hazarded their lives for love of Christ. They were a despised illegal group, and knew that at any moment imperial Rome might attempt to crush them out of existence: yet they refused to compromise, or worship Caesar, or offer pagan sacrifices. They continued to meet for worship even when hounded from pillar to post. They sang praises to the Lord, even when they were being burned at the stake, or torn limb from limb in the arena. They refused to be stamped out. Through each succeeding wave of bitter persecution, their faith and courage grew, and they offered "sacrifices well-pleasing to God".

Missionaries of the eighteenth and nineteenth centuries gave up so much that this world values, in order to reach the four corners of the earth with the Good News of Jesus Christ.

They left behind home and loved ones, undertaking journeys in those days of up to five months, with no possibility of communication or frequent furloughs. They left behind the relative security of western civilisation with its systems of justice, in a time when many other parts of the world were ruled by despotic cruelty. They faced hunger, imprisonments, floggings, often with no knowledge of the crimes of which they were accused, apart from being "foreign devils". They gave up all prospects of the security of a salaried job, accepting often a meagre pittance, in order not to burden a local church with their support. They went where there were no doctors or modern medical science to help them in time of physical need and pain, risking their lives that others might live. They deliberately chose to leave the ease and pleasures amongst which several had grown up, to accept in exchange the rugged hardships of trekking in the jungles in an inhospitable climate, amongst nationals with unknown languages, culture and dietary habits.

All this might be called "*sacrifice*", be it in the first or nineteenth century, in the sense that it was a privileged love-gift to Christ. It was a thankoffering to the Lord, who had loved them, and had given Himself for them. It was their only way to express the depth of their humble gratitude for so great a salvation. Like Peter and the Apostles, they forsook ALL in order to follow Him.

What of us in this twentieth century?

We love the same God. We are bought with the same price. Christ died for our sins as much as for theirs. Are we less willing to be identified with our Lord and Saviour, than they were? Are we more afraid of ridicule or indifference, than they were of the stake or the arena?

Some to-day, in an apparent attempt at greater honesty, would substitute the word "obedience" for the word "sacrifice", saying that there is no sacrifice that we can make: and the only way we can show our love is by our obedience.

"He who has My commandments and keeps them, he it is who loves Me" (John 14: 15, 21, 23).

How much we should lose of challenge by such a change! *Obedience* tends to be a cold, legal word of calculated action: *sacrifice* throbs with life and passion. Certainly the one will inevitably involve the other. Sacrifice can only be worked out by obedience, but obedience will need sacrifice to give it fire and momentum.

To-day it would appear that we Christians prefer to talk of a measure of commitment, the length to which we are willing to become involved, rather than the depths of God's immeasurable love in which we long to become immersed. There is abroad an atmosphere of careful calculation, "thus far and no further", maintaining certain reasonable limits. The carefree abandonment of love that marks the *sacrifices* of Paul, of second-century Christians, of nineteenth-century missionaries, seems sadly lacking. To-day we weigh up what we can afford to give Him: in those days, they knew they could not afford to give Him less than all!

Oh, that we Christians to-day might be set ablaze with love for our Lord and Master so that we too *must* give Him ALL, as did the poor widow, who coming to the treasury "put in two copper coins which make a penny" of whom Jesus said to His disciples: "This poor widow has put in more than all those who are contributing to the treasury. For they all contributed out of their abundance: but she out of her poverty has put in everything that she had, her whole living" (Mark 12: 41–44).

What do I to-day consider to be my most precious possession? The woman in the home of Lazarus had a long-necked flask of pure ointment, worth a workman's annual wage. To her, it was precious. She broke it, and anointed the head of Jesus with the ointment, and the fragrance filled the whole house. She gave what she prized, and He accepted it as a love-gift, calling her action a beautiful thing. (Mark 14: 3–9).

Ointment would not be very precious to me, whatever it cost. But at the present time when the great stress is on "human rights" and the "charter", how many of us have got caught up in the language and attitudes of our day, so that our "rights" really are the most precious thing we possess? My right to be heard, to voice my opinion, to be consulted: my right to make my own choices and decisions as to what I'll do and where I'll do it: my right to be myself, and to be considered as a human being. Can there be anything wrong with such attitudes?

There was nothing wrong with my longing to be a good doctor for the African church and people where I lived; yet God showed me He could better fulfil His plan for them if, at that time, I would be willing to be a sore-handed builder.

There was nothing wrong with my ambition to be a good missionary, with time to talk to the patients in wards and clinics of the love of God: yet God showed me that His purposes would be better served at that time, if I were willing to be an over-worked doctor, a member of a team, where others were given wholly to evangelism.

There is nothing wrong with an appreciation of individual human rights, but perhaps God is asking us to be willing to have a different attitude with regard to ourselves. "My thoughts are not your thoughts, neither are your ways My ways, says the Lord. For as the heavens are higher than the earth, so are My ways higher than your ways, and My thoughts than your thoughts" (Isaiah 55: 8, 9).

*"I appeal to you therefore, brethren, by the mercies of God, to present your bodies as a living sacrifice, holy and*

*acceptable to God, which is your spiritual worship (and your reasonable service)"* (Rom. 12: 1 – RSV and AV).

The Lord is pleading with us for full surrender, an absolute willing sacrifice of all I consider mine, which certainly will include my rights to decide and choose and act on my own initiative. It is not enough to give mental assent to doctrinal teaching. There must be a practical realistic response. The plea is for action. "Present your bodies (all that you are), as a living sacrifice." The Christian is invited to give God all, to make Him indisputably King over every part of life: to become, as it were, His bond slave in total obedience to His will.

My failure to surrender the right to exercise my will to His dominion shows in so many apparently little ways. In the early years at Nebobongo, we had no radios, and so no time signals. We put our watches right by the morning "call-bird" at 5.25 a.m. – but we could all hear a different bird. Then the drum was beaten at 6.20 a.m. for church service at 6.30 a.m.; the five minutes' difference between the pastor's watch and mine could cause real friction. Either I was not quite ready for prayers, or I would be five minutes late for the ward round, and both situations annoyed me. Basically, why? Because I reckoned that I was in charge and had the *right* to know the correct time!

For four years, I have been a deputation speaker for the Worldwide Evangelization Crusade. I have had the privilege of sharing in many different places the needs of the rapidly developing third world church, and the response in prayer and giving has been most generous, though the response in personnel to fill the vacancies has been frequently less marked. The British WEC finance office left me free to channel the finance into those projects and ministries that most burdened my heart round the world. I asked them once to accept more directly this responsibility, as I feared lest I failed to be rightly guided, but they chose to leave me with this freedom. So I pledged a certain total every week of each year to the general support fund for our overseas missionaries, and God graciously honoured this decision.

Then in one country where I was travelling, the WEC national finance office did accept this responsibility of choice, in distributing any finance that was contributed. I simply had to hand it all in, with a list of donors for official receipts. The committee would disburse the accumulated funds at the end of the tour. This was just what I had previously asked for: but because I did not ask for it this time, I objected to its imposition. My pride bristled. Could they not trust me? How perverse could I be? I had not wanted to be burdened with that trust before, and yet now I wanted to retain the right. I wanted the right to say how the money should be used, or to choose to hand it over to the committee. Actually the committee decided on exactly the same policy that I had always maintained, that every possible penny should go to the general support fund for our missionaries round the world: and the weekly target was maintained. BUT – I had lost the right to choose. My pride was hurt.

I'm sure that for me, a "sacrifice well-pleasing to God" is to give Him my will, and thereby my "rights" on all levels. On the same tour of meetings, I heard that a far-reaching decision had been made by our home staff, that very closely affected my own future. I wrote a heated letter, in some resentment that I had not been consulted, and demanding my right to re-consider my appointment to the new programme. As I typed the words: "my right to . . .", I knew I was grieving God, and tore the letter up. We have no rights, but to love and obey Him, to be submissive to His will and utterly loyal to His leadership. The actual "rights and wrongs" of the case were at that moment of secondary importance: He could work them out in His own perfect timing. Just then what mattered was my personal relationship to God, as a *living sacrifice*.

To be a living sacrifice will involve all my time. God wants me to live every minute for Him in accordance with His will and purpose, sixty minutes of every hour, twenty-four hours of every day, being available to Him. No time can be considered as my own, or as "off-duty" or "free". I cannot barter with God how much time I can give to serve Him. Whatever I am doing, be it a routine salaried job, or housework at home, be it holiday time and free, or over-time Christian youth activities, all should be undertaken for Him, to reveal His indwelling Presence to those around me. The example of my life must be as telling as my preaching if He is to be honoured.

To be a living sacrifice will involve all my possessions. Everything I have is in trust, be it financial or material. All should be available to God for the furtherance of his Kingdom. My money is His, if I am to live sacrificially. I must look to Him for guidance in its use, with no sense that a certain percentage is my own, by right of labour. I relinquish that right to Him. He has the right to direct the spending of each penny. My home or my car, my typewriter or my clothes, anything I own is to be considered primarily God's, to be used as He instructs: and even lent to another, should He desire! The acquisition or replacement of material goods should be undertaken in accordance with His will, not as a result of a flight of fancy. I must consider that I own nothing. All is God's and what I have, I have on trust from Him, to be used as He wishes.

To be a living sacrifice will involve all of myself. My will and my emotions, my health and vitality, my thinking and activities, all are to be available to God, to employ as He chooses, to reveal Himself to others. Should He see that someone would be helped to know Him through my being ill, I accept ill-health and weakness. I have no right to demand what we call good health. I've no right even to demand a sound mind, except in so far as this glorifies God. I am to be wholly His. All rights are His – to direct my living so that He can most clearly reveal Himself through me. God has the right, then, to choose my job, and where I work, to choose my companions and friends. The indwelling Holy Spirit can cause me to know God's will, not as a passive robot, highly susceptible to false directions, but as an active fellow-worker, sensitive to His highest purposes. "God is at work in you, both to will and to work for His good pleasure" (Phil. 2: 13).

To be a living sacrifice will involve all my love. My emotions and desires are to be actively dedicated to the Lord, with one burning desire, to worship Him more worthily and to serve Him more whole-heartedly. I relinquish the right to choose whom I will love and how, giving the Lord the right to choose for me. This is not fatalism, but a responsible act of my free will, and I must consciously seek to know His will and direction. I accept His law in His Word as my standard in this, as in all other departments of my life. Whether I have a life partner or not is wholly His to decide, and I accept gladly His best will for my life. I must bring all the area of my affections to the Lord, for His control, for here, above all else, I need to sacrifice my right to choose for myself. I dare not trust myself in this area. God knows that which is in my own best interest, and which will make me more wholly available to Himself for the fulfilling of His perfect law of liberty.

Many of our hymn writers have caught this spirit of abandonment to His Lordship: that only by handing over my so-called "rights" can I know the joyous liberty of the out-working of God's "right" to myself.

Make me a captive, Lord, and then I shall be free:
Force me to render up my sword, and I shall conqu'ror
be.

(George Matheson)

and again:

Take my life and let it be consecrated Lord, to Thee.
Take my will and make it Thine; it shall be no longer
mine.
Take my heart: it is Thine own: it shall be Thy royal
throne.
Take my love: my Lord, I pour at Thy feet its treasure
store.
Take myself, and I will be ever, only, all for Thee.

(Frances Ridley Havergal)

I need to be so utterly God's, that He can use me or hide
me, as He chooses, as an arrow in His hand or in His quiver.
I will ask no questions: I relinquish all rights to Him who
desires my supreme good. He knows best. The reasonable
reckonings of the loud clear voice of common sense will no
longer be the deciding factor. To be known as "men who
have risked their lives for the sake of our Lord Jesus Christ"
(Acts 15: 26), to rejoice as those that "were counted worthy
to suffer dishonour for the Name" (Acts 5: 41), to be listed
with those "of whom the world was not worthy" (Heb.
11: 32–38), will be far greater joy than to have received the
world's approval, amassed the world's wealth, succeeded in
the world's estimation (even that of the Christian world).

This abandonment of love is not necessarily foolhardy,
but it will be willing to appear foolhardy if that is necessary.
To go to serve in the church in tropical Africa without
taking the precaution of prophylactic inoculation against
smallpox and yellow fever, and a supply of antimalarial

tablets could be considered thoughtless foolhardiness, and lead to burdening others with caring for one in avoidable sickness: to stay on and serve in such a place when such necessary prophylactic supplies are exhausted and unobtainable for national as well as for foreigner might well be an act of sacrificial love. To stay in a place of danger after being advised to evacuate, and thereby endangering the lives of others who risk all to rescue one would probably be considered worse than foolhardy: to be caught in the midst of danger, without warning or route of escape, and to behave with quiet dignity in the centre of brutality and humiliation, comforting and encouraging others in the same predicament, can only be seen as sacrificial love. The line between these two will frequently be very fine, and possibly indefinable to an onlooker, who might therefore call thoughtless foolhardiness sacrificial love, and vice versa: but to the Lord God and to His servant it will be clear and distinct.

There will always be problems, where the advice of well-wishers may vary considerably. During my first term of service in Congo/Zaire, the mounting load of work with all its pressures of responsibilities, and resultant weariness, became a major problem for me. Therefore it was mentioned clearly and distinctly in my letters home to those who prayed for me regularly. I shared with them the problem and my need, as I saw it. I needed to sort out priorities every day: I needed clear wisdom as to what to do and what not to do, and in what order to do that which needed doing. I needed to maintain my spiritual life, in close fellowship with my heavenly Father. I needed to see Him shining through the veritable mountain of obstacles in a quiet orderliness. I needed Him to control my irritability, and cause me to know His triumphant graciousness. Only a miracle could achieve this in all the given circumstances. And I looked for that

miracle, through the prayers of faithful loving friends.
Then the letters began coming.

"You must be out of the Will of God. He never over-taxes His servants' strength."

"Surely you are acting in stupid pride, thinking you can do such a gigantic task. Somewhere you have obviously missed God's way for your life."

"Learn to say 'No'. God will get no glory if you break down."

I had wanted prayer fellowship. I had not expected so much criticism. Doubtless many who did *not* write *were* praying: but I had to read the letters of those who *did* write. I was stung and goaded. How could they criticise so heartlessly? What did they know or understand of the real situation where I lived?

"You must guard your quiet time alone with God in the morning, at all costs. Say 'NO' to every interruption."

As soon as I lit the lantern at 5.0 a.m. there would be a knock at the door. They had only been waiting for me to wake, to tell me they needed me urgently in either the general hospital or the maternity compound. A mother needing immediate surgery if her baby were to live – what was I to say? "Come back in an hour and I'll be free then" knowing the baby would be dead? It just did not make sense in our circumstances. So often I was driven into corners where I could not say "NO" and still live at peace with my conscience.

I told God I would get up at 4.30 a.m. but I tried to bargain that He would keep away all callers till 5.30 a.m. The very next day as I got up at 4.30 a.m. and lit the lantern, there was an immediate knock at the front door – an urgent call for immediate surgery. I went, of course. I didn't even pause to think or question. We saved a mother and baby's life by the Lord's enabling.

"You must learn to say 'NO'. You'll be no help to them dead."

Lord, how?

And He poured in more strength, strength sufficient for the needs of each day. I didn't break down or up: I wasn't dead. I *was* working intensely hard and began to question the reasonableness of it. Then the Lord sent another doctor to join the team. We could alternate weekend duties; we could arrange rotating night-calls. I began to sleep more: and I had more opportunities of regular times for prayer and meditation. Strangely enough, all this did not give me more strength, nor more peace. He provided all I needed under each set of circumstances. He had taught me to avail myself of all quiet moments, such as ten minutes' scrubbing up before an operation, to meditate and "practise the Presence" of God. He had deeply enriched my life through the period of stress, learning to trust Him more and rest in Him.

Another problem arose for me through the varied advice of well-wishers with regard to my responsibility to my Mother. When I first went to Africa, Mother did not need me. There were many of the family in and around the home. When I came home five years later, Mother was living alone. Several indicated that I had "done my fair share" and should now stay at home and live with my Mother, taking a job locally. When Mother heard of this, she was adamant!

"Never!" she said, "You are in the Lord's work, and He wants you in Africa. You must never come home for me. Even if I eventually go to an old people's home, I want you where you are. Am I not part of your work out there?"

How true that was! Dear Mother knew each African colleague by name, their wives and children, and prayed for each in their varying needs. We shared everything, all the problems and burdens, as well as the joys and triumphs. Many a time, in her weekly letter to me, a quiet sentence of godly advice has been used to change completely a local problem and bring solution and peace, where before there had been hardness and unrest.

Each parting was harder. After my liberation from the civil war of 1964, we had a year together, and became very closely knit in the Spirit. Mother had suffered for five years, with rheumatoid arthritis. But she was a fighter, and practically forced me back to Africa when the way opened up for our return. Others were very critical that I left her then.

Three years later, a younger sister died: Mother was deeply distressed. About the same time, she fell, and had to go to hospital. From then on, living on her own was obviously impossible. My married brother had come home from South Africa to help make a home for her. My married sisters turned their homes round to make things easier for Mother to live alternately with them. And others, outside the immediate family, wrote and told me how selfish I was to have left Mother to fend for herself when she needed me: and how thoughtless I was to accept so easily the loving sacrifices of others of the family so that I could continue in the work I enjoyed.

Mother wrote regularly: "You are where God wants you. PLEASE do not let my needs get in the way of His working through you there. The needs of your African people are far greater than mine."

Every week (or almost every week) her letters were so cheerful and victorious. Just now and again, a phrase slipped in which told me of the other side of the picture, the pain, the relentless advance of the disease, the dread of packing up and moving on. My heart was terribly torn. I found it so hard to be sure of guidance.

I began to come home every summer during the College holidays for two months, to be with Mother, and so to enable the other members of our family to have their summer holidays with their teenagers. Each summer the same fierce battle raged – should I go back to Africa or stay and give Mother a home? Advice raged equally fiercely on both sides, and complicated the issue of guidance enormously.

Then one summer, something was said, and almost immediately, I knew complete peace. Within two days I knew God had spoken. I arranged to come home in one year. I resigned from my work in Africa, and together we prayed for my replacements. Six weeks before I left Nyankunde, they were there in the job! Everything went so peacefully and in such an orderly way (apart from the final horror of the student strike!). We knew it was indeed God's perfect timing. My heart was filled with peace to be going home, and there was no unbearable heart-break at the thought of leaving the place and people and work that I so loved. All the factors that had to be considered worked together in proving to me that God had spoken the word. Obedience to His will and plan brought joy and peace.

Mother died two years later. Even then some wrote saying that it could all have been so different if I'd come home earlier. How true it is that we can never please everyone – but we *can* always please Him.

Despite the problems involved in the out-working of His Will, what the Lord longs for is our love, our whole-hearted, unmeasured, abandoned love, proved in our obedience. His prayer for us is that we should love.

"A new commandment I give to you, that you love one another; even as I have loved you, that you also love one another. By this all men will know that you are My disciples, if you have love for one another" (John 13: 34, 35).

As He loved us, so we should love Him, that He may love through us all whom He would reach. Christ so loved us that He gave Himself to be the propitiation for our sins, a willing

Substitute, the one perfect sufficient Sacrifice. He left the glory of heaven to come to earth to pay the penalty of our sin, taking our place on the Cross of Calvary, and dying for us, the Just for the unjust, that He might redeem us and bring us to God.

In a response of overwhelming gratitude and love, let us count no cost too great to give to the Lord the service of our lives: through every moment of every day, rendering to Him those *"spiritual sacrifices that are acceptable to God"*.

> Were the whole realm of nature mine.
> That were an offering far too small:
> Love so amazing, so divine,
> Demands my soul, my life, my all.
>
> (Isaac Watts)

Also available in Hodder Christian Paperbacks

# Knowing God
## J. I. Packer

'*The author defends and restates many of the great biblical themes ... he illumines every doctrine he touches and commends it with courage, logic, lucidity and warmth ... the truth he handles fires the heart. At least it fired mine, and compelled me to turn aside to worship and to pray.*'

John Stott, *Church of England Newspaper*

'This book is strong meat. To read and digest it is an experience no discerning reader is likely to forget.'

*Church Times*

'Here is the work of an arresting, even scintillating writer, and strong argument presented with verve and imagination ... A faithful study of this book would lead many Christians into their full inheritance.'

Frank Cumbers, *Methodist Recorder*